Around the Tables

GW00503153

Donal F Shannon

Dedicated to

my sister Claire Dobson

Synopsis

A true story about a group of professional Waiters. Due to divorces, alcohol, gambling and dishonesty have ended up unable to work in full time employment. All these characters walked a tightrope of life. They did not socialise with each other, and neither had much knowledge about each other's background but remained very loyal to each other. Each one dependant on the other. They all, with exception of one, drank a lot, a couple gambled, petty theft that they regarded as perks, worked long hours, each had either troubled a home life or no home life, a bit pathetic in some respects. Life controlled by fears of varying types.

Contents:

CHAPTER 1

AROUND THE TABLES

"How long have you worked here Dan?" asked Martin putting on his dickie-bow.

"I have been here on and off for about two years, so have Mick and Chris. Joan comes sometimes but she can be a bit unreliable if she decides to have a few too many glasses of happiness."

"You seemed to vanish a few years ago Dan, some people thought you were dead."

Martin: "I got a job in a factory as a welders-mate, big boots, overalls the lot. I let my hair grow long and grew a beard, got involved in AA and joined the human race so to speak."

"Why Dan?"

Martin: "my drinking got so out of hand I became unemployable, I was turning up pissed up for jobs, not turning up at all. I once poured white wine in a lady's gin and tonic. I turned up for a job in a posh restaurant with sick all down my Tuxedo."

"I notice you have the beard, but it is very smart and well groomed."

"It is now. Martin: "anyway I got a call from Maria at the Black and White agency asking me if I was thinking of coming back in the business on a casual basis and that she could promise me plenty of work, so I talked it over with Joan and she agreed, only if I would teach her to be a silver-service waitress."

"Is she here today? I haven't seen her in years, has she packed in drinking too?"

"In her case it got worse, I had to come home early from the factory because she was pissed up. That was the reason I taught her to be a waitress so we would work together. The difference being, I used to drink while I was working and she doesn't when she works so I try and get us as much work as possible together. Anyway, how's your family?"

"My wife had an accident and is now in a wheelchair so I have been caring for her and getting some cash-in-hand jobs. I had to leave that head-waiter's job at the Curzon Hotel due to the accident in the car. Come to think of it that was the last time I saw you. You came one busy night to do wines for me. Everyone was looking for you when I noticed the party at table five in the corner had become seven people and there was you, sitting drinking at the table, you were well gone. I had to send you home."

"That's all a long time ago Martin. Come and let's go down to the restaurant and see Mick and Chris. It's a carvery, all we serve is the tea and toast. The lunches are all buffets and the dinners are all carvery. The Restaurant Manager has just gone, he was a right wally. We got him cleaning the carvery and the bay windows. He was laying up the tables for breakfast and we were sitting chilling out in the bar next door called "Maggie's" when Mr Gray, the General Manager, took him aside and told him he didn't need a cleaner or a waiter as he had plenty of them and fired him. There is a new guy starting tomorrow, I wonder how long he will last?"

"Hi Mick, hi Chris, guess who is here?" said Dan.

"Hi Martin, good to see you again it will be like old times again" said Mick.

"Good to see you Mick, I see your hair has not grown since I saw you, and Chris has not changed much - put on a little weight around the belly maybe. You are the same age aren't you? Same birthday I remember, what are you now, 38?"

"How did you remember that Martin" said Chris.

"How could I forget your 38th when we got pissed up at that wedding in the Marquee and I fell over the cake and tore the brides dress, and the agency had to pay for a new cake and you two ended up with the bridesmaids in the bridal suite"?

"You two have been working together a long time now, you worked with Mick in Glasgow and Mick worked with you in Ireland."

"We only have a couple of Aussie tours today and we will have a chat in "Maggie's" after breakfast. Here comes Rachel the supervisor," "Rachel this is Martin."

"You don't know this lot Martin do you? I hope they don't put any bad ideas in your head." said Rachel, a tall, good looking girl, about 25 years old.

"They won't Rachel, I know them, and I'll work with Dan so they don't corrupt me" laughed Martin.

After breakfast the guys make their way round the corner to "Maggie's Bar". When they went in there were a few already there, nearly all catering staff.

"This is Paul the barman, Martin is one of the boys, lets you run up a slate, he is also partial to the odd glass of happiness himself, and what are you having?" laughed Dan.

I'll have a pint of lager Paul and you might as well give them what they want" smiled Martin.

'That's lager for Mick, Guinness for Chris and a Coke for Dan and one for myself, that's an even fiver Martin" said Paul.

"Over here Martin, this is our comer, do you still play pool." shouted Mick.

"Not with you two anyway, last time I played with you I lost £20 and I haven't forgotten" smiled Martin.

"How is your son Nathan doing Martin?" asked Chris.

"He has left catering college now and is working for the Black and White agency at the moment, I will probably bring him with me to the River Gate. He has got a lady friend now and I think he may move in with her."

"He is a good waiter Martin, he is the only one of us to go to catering college" said Mick.

"You still happily married Chris? Asked Martin". "Are your girls still doing Irish Dancing?"

"The eldest won a big competition last week and the wife still loves me" laughed Chris.

"What about you Mick? Still living with that big girl. She was a bit crazy wasn't she?"

"Still is Martin, I don't live with her but I go to see the kids when I can. She came here to work one day and insulted all the punters, calling them stupid. She's banned here thank God." laughed Mick.

"You doing lunch Dan"? Asked Martin.

"Yes, I think we all are. It must be very busy. Here comes Billy and Jean. You know them Martin?"

"Yeah, I know them, Christ! Everyone seems to work here. This bar must make a lot of money Dan."

"I'll give you a lift back home if you like, and we can do a bit of catching up,"

"OK Martin. Hi Mick, I'm going back with Martin after lunch." said Dan.

"OK Dan" said Mick

After lunch Martin and Dan headed off home.

"Mick is beginning to show his age Dan, he is getting a little light on top and putting on some weight. He must be about 11 stone now. His face was getting redder and redder during the lunch today, maybe he is having blood pressure problems."

"Rubbish Martin, he had four cans of Special Brew hidden behind the curtain at the bottom of the restaurant, and he is back in tonight."

"I should know better. It does not seem to slow him up, he is as fast as ever and can still clear a table of 12 with one visit, and he still never talks to the customers."

"That is what he has Chris for - he has plenty of blarney and Mick does the work" laughed Dan.

"Hear who's talking Dan. When you get talking to the punters you forget about the work" laughed Martin.

"I noticed "Harrogate Jackie" was there today. I did not have time to talk to him. He never changes Dan, always immaculate. He must be over 40 now, I worked with him 15 years ago and he does not look any different except, the hair is shorter and greyer and the gold rimmed glasses make him look smarter. He is a top class wine-waiter you know Dan."

"The only wine waiting he does now Martin is with himself" laughed Dan "he doesn't get drunk very often because he is always topping up, he just keeps himself to himself you can always see him with a coffee cup but it is generally ½ coffee ½ brandy."

"I don't live too far from you Dan do you want me to pick you up in the morning."

"I think that would be great Martin. Mick will be relieved, he comes right across town. I'll ring him. Just drop me at the shop I need some cat food" said Dan.

"See you in the morning Dan, give Joan my regards."

CHAPTER 2
MAGGIES BAR

Next morning Martin picked up Dan and they got to the River Gate around 7.00am.

The restaurant was divided into three. Rachel was giving out the stations.

"Come on you two! There is a lot of work to do and we are two short from the Agency again." "Cheer up Rachel, the A Team's here - you've got Mick, Chris, me and Martin, who else would you want? You know we won't let you down."

"Piss off Dan, you are full of shit" laughed Rachel. "I am pleased you lot came, otherwise we would be in deep shit. Our new Restaurant Manager starts today, the boss reckons he is good, he is from Morocco or Tunisia."

"He reckoned the last one was brilliant too, and the one before that." laughed Mick, as he walked past carrying a tray of butters.

"Why don't you take the job Rachel I think you would be good at it. Young 25 year old, attractive. Cheeky and who would you have to help you. We would then have plenty of work because you would ask for us." said Dan. "Do you honestly think so Dan?" "Of course I do." smiled Dan

"Don't listen to him Rachel, he is taking the piss, we don't want you cracking up with stress" said Mick.

"Anyway Chris the word in "Maggie's" is that Mr Gray, the boss, is for the high jump" laughed Dan.

"Maybe you can go for his job Rachel," laughed Mick. "Piss off Mick" said Rachel, getting annoyed. "He will be starting at lunch so I hope you lot are sober when you come back at 12.30pm".

"Would we do that?" laughed Chris. "So what's the procedure Dan, after we do breakfast and the tours have gone"? "Relay for the conference. Lunch at 1.00pm. We put the hot dishes on the carvery and lay all the cold dishes, meats and salads etc. over across at the window, there are about 200 delegates today and they will be in all week."

"Then across to "Maggie's Bar", for an hour before lunch?" asked Martin

"You learn fast Martin have you done this type of job before?" laughed Mick.

"Maggie's Bar" is like an agency, it's where everyone hears about where the work is, who's got sacked, who's left, which manager is ripping off who, and who's knocking who off. If you are looking for cash in hand most head-waiters phone Paul the barman asking who's in, who's sober or not. Anyway let's clear this carvery and get round there" said Mick hurriedly.

The bar was down a couple of steps and straight ahead, Paul the barman could see everyone come in and leave. On one side chefs and porters and the other side waiters, waitresses and out of work barmen. Everyone to their own territory. The only time they talked was at work, or when they had a game of pool or darts. There never was any trouble. Sometimes if Paul won some money on the dogs he would keep the bar open for his special friends who were always waiters, Paul being a waiter himself once. Staff from all the nearby hotels used to hang out there from time to time. New staff all made for "Maggie's". Paul only took messages on the phone except the A Team for whom he had a lot of respect.

"I'll just have a coffee Paul, how about you Martin, coffee?" asked Dan. "Coffee Dan? Coffee? Have you forgotten where we are? You know I have a golden rule, never to drink tea or coffee on licensed premises." "Sorry Martin, is a pint of lager better?"

"That's better" smiled Martin.

"Joan's on the lunch today, bus stops outside, should be here soon, she'll be pleased to see you" said Dan.

"Let's go join the boys, Jackie's here on his own studying the horses." "Hi Jackie"

"Hi, Martin. See you eventually made it here, are you doing lunch in the "River Gate"? I'm down the road in the "Brown's Hotel" today, lunch and dinner, but I'll be in the Gate at the weekend. "How's Nathan? Is he a waiter yet?"

"Yes, and a good one at that Jackie, but he is beginning to like his lager too much." "So what's new? It's all the same deal waiter-booze except for Dan, but he has a wardrobe of 'done it tee-shirts" smiled Jackie.

"How's the pony, any big wins lately?"

"A couple of weeks ago I had a tip from a trainer staying at the hotel, for two horses at York. Both won. I had a double up, I drew £650" said Jackie.

"Did you give it all back yet?" "No I paid some debts, had a few beers, lost the rest, skint again, same result" laughed Jackie, downing a large whiskey. "Must go Martin, early lunch, see you later". "See you Jackie" answered Martin, drinking back his lager.

"Mick, phone, I think it's Rachel", shared Paul. "Hi Rachel, okay, yes, now see you" "We better get across they're coming in early, drink up" shouted Mick.

As the team strolled in Rachel was standing at the door of the Anchor Restaurant with a small, balding, swarthy looking man in morning suit holding a briefcase.

"I wonder if he has got our money in that briefcase" laughed Dan.

"Hello everybody, my name is Mr Baltimo. I am your new Restaurant Manager, I hope to turn this restaurant into the best one in town."

"Hi Chris", whispered Mick, "Haven't we heard that same line from the past three, they must be told what to say by Gary."

"I will meet you all personally after lunch. In the meantime, I will just watch this service and Rachel will supervise." announced Mr Baltimo.

"OK everyone, you know that to do. Gary and Peter you work today with Mick and Chris and don't let them send you into the Chef for a banana bender again. Anne and Carol will work with Dan and Martin at the bottom buffet." "Where's Joan? I thought she was on lunch today" said Rachel

"I'm here Rachel, I'm here, you don't think I would let you down do you? The bus was late. Anyway where do you want me?"

"You look after the carvery, replenishing from the kitchen, and if they give you any grief tell me"

"OK Rachel" said Joan

After lunch Mr Baltimo called everyone together. I am very impressed today for lunch I think we will work well together" he announced.

"We only did a bloody buffet! Just give us our money Rachel and let's get home" said Dan. "We have to collect our son from the child-minder, Martin are we off?"

"See you downstairs for your money boys. Thanks for today".

"We are off Mick. See you tonight. Let's go Joan, did you get any meat off that carvery for our tea? asks Dan. "Of course I did let's go."

"Are you in tonight?" Joan asked Martin.

"No, but Dan is, I'm doing the lunch tomorrow."

"Is this a new car Martin?" asked Joan noticing how clean and new looking it was.

"No it only had 12000 miles on the clock, I look after it." "Are you collecting these Carlsberg Special cans for some charity," laughed Joan.

"How do you think Baltimo will do Martin?"

"How long do you give him Dan?"

"Not long, Joan, we know what the Management are like. Rubbish, Martin, he will have no say. Gary and his assistant manager will make it hard for him. He has no staff only a few students and the Agency. That is why we run that restaurant. They work their students till they drop. They don't do any work themselves, no social skills, but I suppose that is a good thing for us they can't keep staff. They will always need the agency, and while they pay us cash in hand, we will always be at the Gate"

After a couple of weeks poor Mr Baltimo was beginning to show signs of strain.

"Why don't staff do what I tell them" he asked Don "I ask the agency to send me six staff but they send me four. I ask for you and your friends and they say you are on another job. Last Tuesday they send me Jackie.

He walked in at 7.15pm instead of 6.30pm. He was drunk. I had to send him home. They send me two old waitresses who could hardly walk. They began shouting at me, Mr Baltimo. One customer complain the Gateaux was frozen. I go tell chef he tell me to F... off, what do I do Dan, you are a very professional waiter, tell me."

Chris, Mick, Martin and Joan were standing behind Mr Baltimo. Trying to look sorry for him Mick was practically doubled up laughing, "Don't you worry Mr B I will talk with the Agency, things will get better" said Dan trying to keep a straight face. "Anyway you have quite a few booked tonight. Let's get to work."

"Hi Martin, I think Baltimos cracking up, don't let him see you laughing he might jump out the window'* laughed Dan.

"Chris! You won't guess who I've seen at the desk waiting for a table" smiled Joan.

"I don't believe it. It's Mr and Mrs Sherry!" said Chris "what a surprise Mr Baltimo will get tonight, he is putting them at the window, between the young courting couples."

"Whose Mr and Mrs Sherry?" asked Martin. "You'll see Martin, I better serve them" said Chris.

"Good evening Madam I am the new Restaurant Manager, my name is, Mr Baltimo. I am Tunisian, I hope you enjoy your meal tonight, I will leave you in the capable hands of one of our best waiters". This is Chris."

"Hello Chris, nice to see you again". "You know Chris?" "Oh yes, he always looks after us" replied Mr Sherry. "We'll have the usual bottle of Claret Chris, thank you."

"Joan, you know the couple at the window?"

"Lovely couple Martin, try not to stare at them Mr Sherry gets a little upset."

"She looks like she has been a model or an actress. She looks classy, Joan."

About half an hour later Martin came across to Chris. "Chris, I could have sworn I saw that Mrs Sherry at the carvery with a full plate a few minutes ago" said Martin.

"That was her third time up" said Joan "If you watch after she eats the meal she heads off to the ladies and gets sick". "It will be interesting to see what Baltimo does, I have just seen him staring across" said Joan. "She's also had had three bottles of claret."

The young carvery chef, Natalie, didn't look too happy, she spoke to Dan. "Dan, the head chef is going mad in this kitchen. He has hardly any roast beef left. Who let that woman back in, don't tell me; Baltimo, I have just watched my percentage profit go down her throat. Why didn't that Dan tell Baltimo to tell her we were full up?" yelled a furious Johnno the head chef.

The people at the adjoining tables began to get up and leave before finishing their meals.

By this time Mrs Sherry had been up to the carvery six times, each time for a plate of roast beef, a plate of veg and a plate of roast potatoes. By now Mr Baltimo was at his wits end. The chef was waving his fist at him through the kitchen door window. He came across to Mick, who pretended not to notice what was happening.

"Mick, Mick, help me what shall I do?" he said pleadingly. "Go tell her she has had enough". "Are you sure?" "Yeah, maybe she has forgotten how many meals she has had," smiled Mick" she might apologise and split". "OK Mick, I will" and he walked towards the table.

"Excuse me Sir and Madam but with great regret I will have to ask you if you would like to go through to the lounge for your coffee now. I have had several complaints from fellow guests about the amount of food Madam has had from the carvery" said Mr Baltimo with sweat pouring down his neck.

"EXCUSE ME please but what does this say in the paper" replied Mr Sherry sharply

Come to our excellent carvery eat all you can for £8.50 as he handed the newspaper clipping to the shocked waiter.

"Now you can just piss off and leave us to enjoy our meal".

Baltimo came across to Dan and Martin polishing some glasses at the side of the bar. "What so I do now" pleaded Baltimo, "Give the paper clipping to the chef"

Baltimo headed towards the kitchen, there were some angry words and Baltimo came flying through the swing doors.

"I don't think the chef was too impressed" smiled Martin.

After about fourteen trifles Mr and Mrs Sherry headed into the lounge for coffee. On the way past Chris Mr Sherry gave Chris a £10 note.

"Thanks Chris for your excellent service as usual see you soon". "They were the last to leave and there was no sign of Mr Baltimo.

"Where is the main man, Joan?" asked Mick. "I think he is in his office go and see" said Joan. "The doors locked" shouted Chris but I think he is in there, Mr Baltimo are you there. It's me Chris".

'With that the door opened and an ashen face Baltimo emerged.

"Is that chef gone? He said he was going to kill me."

"Don't worry he is gone and so are Mr and Mrs Sherry, so you can come out here now and go get our money ready, we will be set up for breakfast soon"

"OK, OK I go sort it out thanks Chris." With that he hurried off.

"You should have told him about Mrs Sherry Dan" said Mick.

"That lady has an illness, bulimia I think it's called, and it is not her fault." said Dan "I hope she gets better she is a lovely lady."

"You know she had her own carvery and was banned by her husband to eat there" laughed Chris "You only wanted to get at the chef, it was his advert."

"Serves him right, he would not give us any grub the other night, and he caught me nicking a roast spud and he threatened to cut my hand off."

"That chef does not like you Dan, what have you done tn him, form the first day you walked into the kitchen he has been on your case" said Mick.

"I honestly don't know" answered Dan.

"I could not help but hear what you said Mick, it's obvious," said Martin. "You know the power thing between chefs and waiters?"

"Yeah so, I'm no threat to him"

"Why do you think head chefs grow beards it's because it's a case of 'I can grow a beard in my kitchen and you can't grow a beard in the restaurant', how many waiters do you know have beards? Only one, Dan. That's why he don't like you it's like putting two fingers up to him."

"Thanks Martin, I never thought of that. He will have to shave his off then, won't he" laughed Dan. "Anyway let's get set up for breakfast and get home, I'm shattered."

Next morning about 10am Rachel got a phone call.

"For those who are interested I have just had a call from Mr Gray, to inform me that Mr Baltimo will not be back, he is not well and is returning to London."

"Oh dear, dear" smiled Mick.

"Another one bites the dust" said Chris.

"I hope he takes that bloody chef with him" laughed Dan.

CHAPTER 3
PACO

"Martin, I just thought I would give you a call to ask if you had heard of a Spanish waiter called Paco. Marie from the Agency has asked me to pick him up tomorrow morning for breakfast, she said you know him."

"I know him Mick, he worked with me a couple of times, good waiter, always smiling, very good English, he is about 25 or 26 years old, slight build about 5.7", black curly hair, you can't miss him, he will be standing on the kerb, I nearly run him over twice."

"Does he drink Martin?" "Yeah, quite partial to the old Special Brews". "So what's new he won't be on his own." "He is a typical mystery man, they just seem to appear from nowhere, work for a while then vanish."

"I will see you in the morning Martin, at the Gate, I'm picking up Chris." "I'm picking up Dan at 6.30am, see you in the morning" replied Martin.

"That must be him Mick, on the comer with the umbrella."

"I think you're right Chris, I'll pull over around the corner."

"It's not often you see a waiter with an umbrella." laughed Mick.

"You Paco?" asked Mick "Paco the waiter?" "That's me, Paco the waiter you must be Mick?"

"Get in the back, what's with the umbrella? It's not raining" asked Chris. "I always bring it, just in case" answered Paco.

"How long have you been over here Paco?" asked Chris. "About three years in England, mostly in London, I have only been up here a couple of months."

"I'm Mick and he's Chris. You done much work for Maria, Paco?" "A few jobs, I worked with Martin, Maria said he will be here today." "He told me you like a few beers Paco." smiled Mick.

"I like a few beers. That Martin likes a few beers, I worked on a wedding with him and he drank more than the whole top table together" laughed Paco.

"Where abouts do you live Paco" asked Mick

"I've got a mobile home parked near where you picked me up, my girlfriend lives with me she works as a model."

"Hi Rachel, we have brought a new waiter for you, Paco, this is our favourite supervisor" said Chris.

"Hello Rachel, I'm Paco, it will be nice working with such a pretty lady." "Piss off Paco, typical waiter, full of shit. You can work with those two students on that Aussie tour, they will show you what to do. Mick, Chris, you look after those Japanese in the bottom half."

"That Paco works hard Chris, he seems to be getting on well with those Aussies."

"He has those two students moving a lot faster Mick."

"I see Martin and Dan have just arrived again. Look at the relief on Rachel's face Chris, she is so used to having staff knock."

"I see you have a new recruit Martin?"

"You mean Paco, he's Spanish, we will have to have some commission on all this business we bring you Paul."

"He can sure knock back the pints of lager Martin, he was in here the other night with some girl, they were sitting over in the corner kissing and cuddling all night, when they left they were both pissed up" said Paul "he forgot his umbrella but he was here first thing next day looking for it, he looked like he had won the lottery when I gave him it."

"He takes it everywhere, even when the sun is shining, what was the girlfriend like?"

"A bit rough Martin, a bit rough" said Paul.

"I don't see him Chris can you?" asked Mick.

"We better give him a few minutes Mick, we are a bit early."

"What do you think of him Chris? Dan seems to think he is not all he seems."

"I find him okay, always gives me a couple of pounds for the lift in the morning, buys the lager in "Maggie's" and gets on well with the punters, Rachel likes him."

"Here he comes now Chris."

"Sorry I'm late, woman trouble" said Paco "she doesn't like me leaving her alone." "Why don't you bring her with you Paco?"

"She has not done it before" said Paco. "Just phone Maria, tell her she is a waitress bring her tomorrow! We will cover for her. All she needs is a white blouse and a black skirt." "OK. I'll phone her after breakfast to tell her" said Paco.

Next morning Paco was waiting on his own at the corner pick up spot.

"Where is she then Paco? Are you scared we might steal her?" laughed Mick. "She is in for lunch at 11.30 today. She has to buy a white blouse and skirt. I told her to meet me in "Maggie's" and I will take her to the Gate." said Paco.

"We are not busy anyway for breakfast but we have a lot of buffets for lunch. All she will have to do, is stand behind the buffet table and collect plates" said Chris.

"Hi Paco; your lady friend is over in the corner, you owe me for a large G&T. She said you would pay when you came in" said Paul.

"That's okay Paul. Here's a tenner get the boys a drink, they are coming behind me.

"Hello darling Glad you made it. Want another drink?"

"Just a small one Paco. Come over here and give me a love."

"Here look after my umbrella Chantelle."

"Cheers Paco" said Martin sipping his lager. "Aren't you going to introduce me?"

"This is Chantelle the love of my life."

"Hi Chantelle! I'm Martin, here comes Dan with Mick and Chris. Dan's the one with the orange juice."

"I'm feeling a bit nervous, I haven't done it before."

"Don't worry it is only buffets today. All you do is stand behind the buffet table and smile" laughed Mick.

"There is a little more to it than that Chantelle, but don't worry we will keep an eye on you" smiled Chris.

"Martin, have you got a minute?"

"Yes Paul, what's the problem?"

"I didn't want to say anything to you in front of Paco."

"Go on. What is it? He can't hear us - he is in love."

"There were two right shady characters in here last night asking about Paco."

"What did they say?"

"They wanted to know where he worked. I told them I did not know. They had a couple of drinks then left, but the tall one said they would be back tonight."

"What did they look like Paul"?

"They were certainly not from around here, or waiters. The tall one looked shifty.

Smart casual clothes, southern accent, short hair .The smaller one was black, Adidas track suit, expensive watch, big thick gold chain and bracelet."

"I'll tell him after lunch, you say nothing to him Paul."

"Rachel, this is Chantelle she has not worked in hotels before. She is Paco's girlfriend" said Martin.

"We have a lot of buffets today, Chantelle, you can look after the buffet in the York suite. The guys will show you the ropes."

"Where can I put my jacket?"

"Put it under the buffet table, so you can keep an eye on it." Said Mick.

"Paco, you work in the Booker suite with Martin and the rest of you stay in the main restaurant. Okay let's go guys start bringing the food out and get set up. The conference will be in at 1.00pm, we only have 45 minutes."

"Chantelle you just stay in the York suite and the guys will bring your food in. The plates, napkins and cutlery are already there."

"Chris I have just brought some salads into the York suite. You want to nip in and see Chantelle's new blouse!"

"What's wrong with it Dan?'

"Go and see for yourself Chris! Bring some stuff through for the buffet."

"Chantelle" whispered Chris "I think you should have a long sleeved blouse."

"What's wrong with my tattoos?"

"Nothing, but the boss might not be too keen! Anyway I will bring the rest of your stuff and get back to my buffet, they will all be in in a minute."

"Does Paco know about his girlfriend's blouse Dan?" "You better tell him Chris. Rachel will send her home. Here he comes now, Paco I think Chantelle could do with some help in the York suite".

"Okay, I'm on my way Chris."

"Chantelle, why didn't you buy a long sleeved blouse?" "Because the shop did not have any Paco and anyway you did not tell me this place was posh!" "You stupid or something? Buying a short sleeved blouse and your arms covered in tattoos!" "Don't call me stupid you Spanish git or I'll punch your head in." "But Chantelle I love you". "Love me, your arse! I'm off to the pub I'll wait for you there. You can tell that Rachel to stick her job where the monkey stuck his nuts."

"What's the matter* what's all the shouting about in here." "It's alright Mr Gray, it's my girlfriend, and she is not too well. She is going home." "There is nothing wrong with me. It's him, he does not like my tattoos, don't you, I am going back to my old job. I earn more for a short time than you were going to pay me for four hours."

"Rachel, I want that girl off the premises now, and not to come back here again."

"Very well Mr Gray, Paco will you ask your girlfriend to leave;."

"Are you coming Paco? I'm off."

"Hi, what about our money Rachel."

"I will give it to Mick for you."

"Tell him I'll see him in "Maggie's.""

After lunch the team headed for "Maggie's".

"Dan, Look what I found, Paco forgot his umbrella."

"Let me see that Martin". "What are you doing Dan?" "I'm trying to open it."

"Give it here Dan. I'll show you what's this? It's a zip. It's like a wallet or a purse and it's full of little packets of white powder."

"Show me that's coke. There must be about thirty packets here, holly shit! Paco must be a dealer." "What are we going to do Dan?" "Well there is one thing certain I am not bringing this into "Maggie's", you go ahead and I will get rid of the umbrella. If he asks about its say it wasn't there it probably got nicked."

"Dan, Paul told me that two shady guys were in the bar last night looking for Paco, now we know why. I better tell him but I won't mention the umbrella."

"Two pints lager, one pint Guinness and a coke Paul, and one for the love birds in the corner."

"I think they have had enough Martin. They have been causing some bother over there with those chefs. I have had to tell them to cool it a few times."

"Alright Martin, my good friend - come and sit with us. We are a bit pissed."

"I'm going to the toilet Paco, get me another drink."

"Paco, where did you meet Chantelle?" "She was a hooker, I fall in love. That's why I try to make her a waitress". "I don't think you will succeed unless she gets those tattoos off, or she gets a new blouse."

"I have got to go back over, I forgot my umbrella."

"Paco, there were two guys in here looking for you last night."

"What did they look like, one black guy and one white?"

"Same two, said they would be back tonight, I think they were from London."

"Oh shit! Wait till I tell Chantelle, I must go get the umbrella, I left it under a table."

"I have just seen Paco running up the steps at the Gate."

"You have Dan, he is gone back for his umbrella, said Martin" smiling.

"Where is Paco?"

"He has just nipped across for his umbrella Chantelle."

"What do you mean his umbrella? It's my umbrella, he just looks after it for me, in case I need it when it rains."

"Where is it then?" "It's gone! It has not been handed in. Somebody's nicked it."

"You stupid bastard! I'm off and you can piss off!" said Chantelle grabbing her coat and running out of the bar.

"I'm in deep trouble! See you guys. I'm off!" said Paco who by this time was as white as a sheet.

"What did you do with the umbrella Dan?"

"Just slung it in the skip Martin."

"Hi Mick did you see her face when I said it was Pace's umbrella, maybe Chantelle was the dealer, and Paco was just looking after it for her."

"Do you know all the years we have been together, I can't think of any of us, or our close circle of waiter friends taking drugs". "Years ago I smoked a little dope Chris, so did Mick, but never took pills or anything else." "I think there is no substitute for Special Brew Dan". "Speak for yourself Mick! I substitute life".

"He seemed a good guy but I don't think we will see him again Martin, do you?"

"Not if those two guy's see him first, the tall guy, Paul said, looked a nasty piece of work."

"Listen are we off I'm tired, I had to do their work as well as my own Martin". "Okay let's go, see you lot in the morning, I will need some petrol money Dan, and you haven't given me any money for a while." "Sorry Martin, here's a tenner that should cover it, let's go."

CHAPTER 4
PABLO AND PEDRO

Next Monday when the guys arrived at the hotel, Rachel greeted them with a big smile.

"Good morning guys! I have some good news for you! We have a new Restaurant Manager and Headwaiter starting today."

"Rachel, you mustn't laugh when you tell us such good news. Are you not expecting them to stay?"

"When you meet them, you will realise why I am laughing Mick. And, I have another bit of news for you - but keep it among yourselves! Mr Gray is for the high jump."

"About time Rachel, does he know?"

"Oh yes, he is being transferred down south but where he is going is a dump."

"Like here Rachel."

"Don't be like that Chris."

"I'm only joking Rachel, we like it here and especially working for you."

"Who do you think you're kidding Chris, we are about the only place left who pay cash in hand after every shift."

"You know I don't get any money Rachel, all my money goes to the Waiters Benevolent Fund for destitute waiters, waitresses and chamber-pots. Martin is the treasurer."

"Pull the other one Dan it's got bells on. Right you lot, there is three tours this morning, and I have only three of my own staff, two knocked again."

"Yesterday was pay day wasn't it Rachel? It is always the same. They get pissed and can't get up. You don't appreciate us like you should."

"Shut up Chris! You can look after the carvery and make sure you don't go walkabout, I have these Aussies shouting at me about no bacon, no sausage, and no eggs."

"Why didn't they make you head waitress Rachel instead of this new guy, you have been here a while, you know the score, you know all the couriers, now you will lose the brown envelope with the tips in."

"What brown envelope Mick?"

"Rachel don't come the innocent with us, we know the score, we have seen the courier slip you the envelope full of money, what is it now 50p or £1 a head?"

"Oh, that brown envelope". That gets handed into the reception and is shared out amongst the staff."

"Yes, that envelope Rachel. Why don't we get any? We do all the work."

"You're casual staff. Only the full time employees get tips, Chris."

"Leave it Chris! Get the food out, it is nearly 7.00 am, and you know those tours are in on the dot"

"O.K. Dan, I'm on the job"

"Let's get back over, we don't want to be late for our new boss on his first day Mick."

"OK Chris, let's go. Hurry up Dan. Martin were off over."

"We'll be over in a minute Mick."

"Hi" Gather around everybody. I would like you to welcome Pablo, our new Restaurant Manager and Pedro his head waiter, I hope they will get all your support."

"Thank you Rachel, I am Pablo, and this is Pedro, and before we start we are gay - as if you had not guessed already, and I intend to make this Restaurant the best in town."

"Now where and who said that before?" whispered Chris.

"Nearly every previous Restaurant Manager that has been here and we know what happened to them, Mick."

"Where are Martin and Dan? Mick?"

"Here they come now, Rachel."

"Come on you two and meet Pablo and Pedro."

"Well what do you know! Martin and Dan it's good to see you."

"Nice to see you two again, still together, I thought you had split up Pablo."

"He could not live without me Dan."

"Don't flatter yourself Pedro, without me he would have got lost, Dan."

"Are you working this lunchtime Pablo?"

"No, we just called in to introduce ourselves. We start officially next Monday, but I am pleased to find you here. Do you work for the Hotel, or are you still doing Agency work Martin?"

"We come through the Black and White Agency. Maria, you remember her? She sends us here most days. As you can see there are not many full time staff."

"So I am led to believe Martin. I will call in to "Maggie's" after you finish and we will have a chat and meet the rest of the team. Anyway we will get off now, and let you get on with your work."

"See you later Pablo."

"OK, everybody, the conference finishes in twenty minutes, let's go, chop, chop."

"Rachel, wait a minute until you see those two performing."

"How do you know them Dan?"

"That would be telling Rachel, but I can tell you they are both good, Pablo is the total extrovert and Pedro the worker, you will find out."

"He just looks like that guy; or should I say gay .that used to be on TV. Russell Grant"

"Wait until you see how he dresses Rachel."

"Hi Dan, how come you know the two P's."

"I worked with Pablo years ago in the Lake District, Martin and I worked with them in Blackpool when we used to go and work on weekend conferences. Pablo was always the boss and front man, and Pedro the worker. They will do well here Mick, they are both very clever. Funny thing is they have plenty of money."

"Dan I never told you about when I first met them. About 10 years ago, I saw a job advertised in the "Caterer" magazine for a wine waiter in a country hotel in the Peak District."

"Stop gossiping and get back to work you two."

"Okay Rachel, I will tell you in "Maggie's" Dan, Pablo said he would meet us there after lunch."

"Your two friends are over in the corner Martin" smiled Paul as he poured Martin a pint of lager.

"Hi barman the drinks are on me and have one yourself."

"Cheers Pablo, and the barman's called Paul a friend of ours."

"Sorry Paul, have a large scotch on me."

"You go sit down Mick I'll bring the drinks over."

"Thanks Paul, the big one is our new boss and the smaller one is Pedro, his partner, his second in command."

"This is Mick and Chris, we also go back a long time Pablo, I had just been telling them about the first time I worked with you two in that country house hotel."

"Stop laughing Pablo! I was the one who ended up in hospital."

"Sorry Pedro, I know it was not funny at the time, but it was later."

"Tell us what happened Pablo, I'll get the drinks, give us a hand Chris."

"It was called "Rodley Manor" near Buxton and I was the head waiter and Pedro was the waiter. The manager's wife ran off with the wine waiter. He took to his flat at the top of the building in a deep depression and I ended up running the place I needed a new wine waiter. That's when I put an advert in the "Caterer" for a wine waiter, and Martin turned up."

"I had to walk about three miles up this narrow road till I came to this big house, it looked like one of those big houses in those Dracula movies. It was late, as I had got off the bus in the village and called into the local pub till closing time.

"I was behind the reception when he arrived, he had a skinful. I got Pedro to show him his room."

"I came down in the morning, Pablo here showed me around. I thought he was the owner. He explained to me we were not going to be too busy,

The Chef was French, I thought he was the kitchen porter.

"The menu was very limited, because the owner had not paid his bill to the major suppliers, so everything was on a cash-on-delivery service."

"One of the first things Pablo asked me, was if I could ride a bike. I wondered why, but I said no anyway. I was soon to find out."

"Martin asked me to show him the wine cellar, so I showed him it. I will always remember his face when I told him it was empty. When the customers asked for wine with their order, I sent Pedro to the local village Off Licence on the bike."

"One Saturday night he sent me five times! On the last time, I was knackered and I turned a bend too fast, crashed into a tree and broke my wrist, and ankle and by the time I got back to the hotel all I got out of Pablo was 'were is the wine? The customer is going mad, I was in pain - he wasn't bothered.

"The next day he tried to teach Martin how to ride the other bike."

"I fell off twice, I thought if it ever gets out about me becoming a mobile wine-waiter, I would never live it down. So I went upstairs packed my gear, said my fair-wells and went home."

"The chef left the next day". The boss's wife came back, he came downstairs, forgave her and we left. As we were going down the drive, Pedro shouted back to his wife, "I hope you can ride a bike".

"We must be off home Pablo", "see you at work tomorrow."

"We are off ourselves. We have just bought a large house in the other side of town and we have the builders in. See you all tomorrow."

CHAPTER 5
THE WEDDING

"Hi Dan, Maria here. You're a hard man to find these days. I have a big wedding coming up on Saturday and they have just rung me for staff. I know its short notice.

I am sending 20 staff and I want you to run it."

"Where is it Maria?"

"It's near Harrogate in a marquee. You might know the groom, Ronnie Jones."

"Not the Ronnie? Getting married? I wouldn't miss it!"

"I will phone you tomorrow with the details, I must ring around for more staff. Bye."

Dan phoned Martin to tell him about Maria's call.

"Did Maria ring you about the wedding?"

"Just now, I have put the phone down."

"Did she tell you whose wedding it is?"

"Yeah, Ronnie Jones, this should be some wedding Dan. She has asked me to do the bar. You're in charge of the reception. I think all the team will be there. There is nothing on at "The Gate" anyway."

"Can you remember the last job we did for him at that night club, his 50th birthday party? Everyone was pinning £50 notes on his jacket, and he whispered in your ear he was 48."

"Do you want to pick me up Saturday morning on your way?"

"OK Dan, see you later."

When Dan and Martin arrived at the wedding venue a large marquee was erected next to a big house up a winding lane.

"Some place this. Where is everybody, have we got the right day?"

"Let's have a look around Martin".

"Your name Dan?"

"No, he is Dan."

These two rough looking guys in jeans, big boots, gold chains, t shirts, with bulging muscles standing against a portable bar.

"My name's Ronnie. It's my wedding and this is Davy my best man. Maria said you would be in charge Dan, if everything goes well, there will be a good drink in it for you."

"What time are you getting married Ronnie?"

"4 o'clock, so we should be back here about 5.00 p.m. everything will be ready I hope."

"No problems. Martin here is in charge of the bar, and I will be at the top table during the meal."

"Good. Now I want you both to come with me, I want to show you something."

Ronnie led the two men on a guided tour.

"This is my house, soon to become my wife's house. Let's go down to the cellar, there are three fridges here. The one across there is special, all the bottles of champagne in there are not to be given to all the guests, only the special guests, I will point out to you later. These two fridges contain white wine and a more common brand of champagne. You can clear these two fridges completely. Over there, are several boxes of brandy and gin, you can also give all that to my guests. But over in the corner there is 5 star brandy - just for myself and special guests."

"Now have you got all that. Give everybody as much as they want, except the good stuff. I am off now, so I will see you later. The food will be arriving about now, check I am not being ripped off."

"Dan, have you seen the amount of stock he has here, and he wants it all given away! I better get mine in the car now while there is no one around!"

With that Martin filled a box of good brandy and champagne and took it upstairs and into the boot of his car. He then proceeded to erect a bar, under the awning attached to the side of the house. Dan just turned a blind eye and went to talk to the catering company arriving with the food.

"Hello, I'm Dan. I'm in charge of this Wedding. You must be the head chef."

"Yes, I'm Nick and this is my second Chris, we have a hell of a lot of food, very expensive food at that. This guy who is getting married must be very rich."

"Yes he is," answered Dan, thinking if they only knew! Ronnie was the top bad guy in the area, who had a finger in all sorts of shady businesses.

"Is there anywhere we can get a drink around here before we get set up?"

"Go see Martin over there, he will fix you up. Ask him for a couple of large Napoleon XL. He'll know what you mean."

Dan counted the tables in the big marquee, 20 in total and the top table of 12. So with 10 around each and top 12 that was 212.

Just then the staff began to arrive. Jackie came with Joan, Billy and Jean. Chris and Mick came in one car, and then about 12 girls from Maria's - some Dan knew and some he didn't. Dan called everyone into the small tent.

"Good morning everyone, nice to see all those happy faces so early. For those who don't know me, my name is Dan. I am in charge today, so let's make it a good job. It will be a long day, but you will all be getting paid when we finish. I will be doing that, so if you see me heading down that lane by myself at about 10.30 p.m., you will know you are not getting paid," laughed Dan.

"Jackie, you and Joan are on the top table. Tables 1 - 10 Chris, Mick, Billy, and Jean. Tables 10 - 20, Anne, you and your team. Okay?"

"It is only a buffet but there is some hot food as well, rice, potatoes and jacket potatoes. After the meal I want everything off the tables and ash trays on. Any dirty glasses all out the back in boxes. Any complaints see me, don't try and sort anything yourselves - the punters today are not the type to discuss anything."

"Right, there is an urn of coffee and one of tea in the corner, so let's go."

"Jackie, Joan, Mick and Chris, I want you to help Martin to get ready trays of drinks and Sherries and serve them in the reception area on arrival."

"Dan, what's the lay up on the tables?"

"Chef, what's the starter?"

"Prawn cocktail Anne, they will come on plates not glasses, so a small knife and fork will do."

"After the starter I will bring the top table to the buffet. The bride will want to show off her dress. Then one table at a time. Joan, serve the top table sweets, but the rest can go to the buffet. Jackie you can give Martin and myself a hand with the champagne toast. After the sweet I will invite the bride and groom up to cut the cake and pose for photos. Mick, you will take the bottom tier out the back, cut the cake into small pieces to put on plates for the girls to put on with the coffee, and then the speeches begin. You can all go into Martin's bar for a drink on the groom. Okay, any questions?"

"Right, let's go."

"Martin, you all ready on your side?"

"Sure Dan, sure."

"Okay everybody, here they come 45 minutes late. Big smiles."

"Congratulations Mrs. Jones, anything you require Joan here will get it for you."

"Thank you, it's been wonderful."

"Mick," whispered Dan, "do you recognise anyone?"

"Not half, the whole of Yorkshire's Mafia are here, look at who is under those top hat and tails."

"I recognise a few."

"I know most, Harry sent me to work in a club they use, and there are a lot of heavy people here today. I have a bad feeling about this wedding Dan."

"Don't tell me that Mick, I can do without grief today."

"The bride is about 22, Ronnie is about 45. He wants to catch himself on Dan."

"Do you want to tell him Mick?" laughed Dan.

"Joan wants a word Dan."

"Okay Mick, I'll be over in a minute, make sure the Bucks Fizz is flowing."

"Yes Joan, what is it?"

"There is only the bride's mother and father, that little old couple over there, and the bride's sister, that is the only people from her side. The rest look like a load of hoodlums Dan."

"They are Joan, they are."

The meal went well, Dan made the bride and groom happy with his quick wit and excellent timing. The bride's father and mother just sat in complete awe at the whole thing. When the cutting of the cake came Ronnie was as proud as punch, smiling at his young bride. Then the speeches began. One after the other of Ronnie's henchmen gave a speech thanking Ronnie for a great day and thanking him for what he had done for them in the past, how he had looked after their families while they were in jail, how he had visited them, when they were in jail with him and how lucky his bride Caroline was to have met him.

Martin and Jackie decided to make some money for themselves and when a table in the corner asked Martin if he had any special champagne or better brandy his reply was:

"Oh yes, but I will have to charge you a fiver a bottle."

"Just keep bringing it", came the reply.

That was it, the private stock soon disappeared, but Martin kept a few for Ronnie and his special guests that included a couple of ex-CID men friends of his. Of course after the meal and people were floating between tables someone recognised one of these CID men, as someone who had put him away and all hell broke loose. Bottles flying, tables overturned, women screaming, and then Ronnie got on the microphone and everyone stopped fighting.

All the staff were terrified and Dan called them altogether.

"Listen everybody, it's just after ten, I want you to get all the plates and coffee cups that aren't broken cleared away and help those chefs get their stuff onto the wagons at the back. Then I will get the money and we can get out of here. Okay."

With that everyone went about their work. About twenty minutes later this Irish waitress called Anne came to Dan practically crying.

"What's the matter Anne, we will all be gone in about half an hour."

"I have just met a guy in the car park who said we were not being paid."

"Rubbish Anne, who told you that?"

"Him over there at the bar with that other guy."

"That's the groom Anne, he was joking. I'll sort it."

Dan noticed they had both changed.

"Hi Davy, could I have a word?"

"Sure Dan," coming across to Dan, "what's the problem?"

"Anne the waitress has just told me we are not being paid."

"Come over, see Ronnie."

"Ronnie, Dan's just told me about not paying the staff."

"That's right Davy, I went for a walk in the car park and saw her loading a big whack of cheese and about 10lb of beef and pork into her car. She didn't recognise me because I had changed my clothes."

After a deep discussion Ronnie handed over a wad of twenty-pound notes in an elastic band to Dan, they shook hands; Dan nodded to Martin behind the bar. Martin came around and headed in the small tent where all the staff had congregated. Anne was still upset but Dan handed her £250 and said:

"Here Anne, pay your girls and let's get out of here. The rest of you meet

Martin and I in the George about a mile down the road and I'll pay you. Where's Jackie?"

"I saw him in the other tent."

"Go get him Joan."

Joan headed off to look for Jackie.

"Any food you're taking, get it now, we are off. The George closes at 11.00 p.m., we have twenty minutes."

"Hi Dan, can you get someone to give me a hand with Jackie?"

"What's the matter with him?"

"He is as drunk as a skunk, he is brushing the grass in the other tent, I can't get the brush off him, all he keeps saying is, "I can't leave this kitchen floor in this mess." He has a bottle of brandy sticking out of his pocket."

"Mick, Chris, get him in the car."

"Let's go."

"Are you not saying farewell to the bride and groom Dan?"

"You must be joking Martin."

With that they ail headed down the lane, past people carriers and Mercedes all stuck in the hedges of the dirt track. They reached the George with 10 minutes to spare, Dan got the drinks in and they all stretched out knackered. Martin called Dan up to the bar.

"Dan, what did you say to Ronnie Jones to change his mind and pay up? I heard him say to Davy, "that was a bit of luck catching that waitress with the cheese, now I can get away with not paying them. I'll tell them the agency will pay them on Monday," and then they started laughing. You came along, whispered in his ear and he turns to Davy, says something and Davy handed him a wad of money and he gives it to you."

"I knew what he was trying to do. I just reminded him of his reputation as a top man and it wouldn't do him any good if people heard he didn't pay for his wedding."

"Rubbish Dan that would not have bothered Ronnie."

"Well actually, I did mention that the Irish waitress was from Belfast, and that her husband was rumoured to be connected to one of those crazy gangs and a top hit-man and he did not need that type of aggravation."

"Is he?"

"I don't know, but it worked," laughed Dan, "and another thing Martin, I will expect my cut of your little scam with selling Ronnie's brandy, you know I see everything."

About a month later Martin phoned Dan.

"Dan, remember Ronnie's wedding?"

"How could I forget it Martin."

"Well have I got news for you."

"Go on then, tell me."

"You remember all that stock, brandy and champagne, the marquee, the catering company who supplied all those king prawns and caviar? "Yes I do."

"Well Ronnie only paid them with bouncy cheques and bent credit cards. Maria did not even get paid her fee for the staff. You were the only one to get any money out of him. Anyway, how much did he give you for yourself?"

"Shit happens, Martin, shit happens. About my tip, I do remember sending a donation to the Waiters Benevolent Fund for Destitute Waiters."

"Dan I never did find out who ran that fund and who was the Treasurer? "Me Martin, me."

CHAPTER 6
HARRY

"How's your new Restaurant Manager doing Dan?"

"He's doing well Paul but you have got to give him time - he has only been there a month, what do you think Mick?"

"Paul, it is like a cabaret show at night, I was working the other night and Pablo was dressed in a black shirt, pink matching dickie-bow and cummerbund and black trousers, you can just imagine him, you've seen him, he's just like Russell Grant, he just waddles around like a duck."

"We seem to get more shifts for dinners since he has come Mick."

"That's right Chris, Pablo knows what he is doing. The evening staff aren't much cop, with us there he can do more posing."

"How about you Martin?"

"Don't forget I know him, his is very clever he is doing well, poor Pedro is running all day long with those big trays, always complaining about Pablo doing his "poseur.""

"He is paid to manage not do any work Martin."

"Chris try telling that to Pedro."

"Dan, I nearly forgot, there was a guy in here last night looking for you, I told him you would be in today after lunch, and he left his number."

"What did they call him Paul?"

"Harry Green"

"Don't know any Harry, do any of you?"

"I know him Dan, he only came on the scene a couple of years ago. I met him at the Agency one day and Maria sent me on jobs with him to do some Christmas parties.

What a man! You think you're good at bullshit. You ought to work with this guy. I wonder what he wants with you Dan."

"I'll give him a ring when I get home Mick, give me his number."

"What is certain Dan, whatever he wants it will only be to benefit to him. This guy has got a code he works with, me first, me second, photo-finish me third. Don't get me wrong, I liked him, he is always asking questions about business. He told me he had a house worth £100,000, he forgot to mention it was a 4 bedroom council house and he was the tenant, even when he is lying he is lying, as long as you remember that. He is likeable."

"Hi, my name is Dan, is Harry there please?"

"Harry there is someone called Dan on the phone."

"Hi Dan, this is Harry Green, thanks for phoning. Is there a possibility we could meet? I have a proposition for you."

"To do with what? Harry."

"I am starting an agency Dan and I need some professional help that is where you come in."

"I'll be in "Maggie's Bar" after breakfast tomorrow about 11.30am and we will have a chat."

"Thanks Dan, about 11.30 then, see you later."

"Who is Harry? Dan we don't know any Harry do we?"

"We do now, Joan, he has worked with Mick and he wants to start an agency and he wants to pick my brains."

"What brains Dan, you had better be careful, if Maria gets to know we will get blown out."

"Sorry I'm late Dan but the car wouldn't start."

"That's okay Martin, Rachel will be delighted for us to just turn up. They are so short of staff."

"Did you get in touch with that Harry last night?"

"Yes, I did I rang him. He wants to start an agency, what do you think?"

"Dan, there is a need because Maria has it all tied up, see what he says anyway, but remember what Mick said about him."

"Anyway, Mick will be there so he can sit in and listen."

"Hurry up you two, I suppose the car broke down again. Dan you work the bottom end with the two students and Martin you look after the carvery."

"Did you see Harry, Dan?"

"No Mick, I talked to him on the phone, he is meeting me at 11.30 in "Maggie's" he will be surprised to see you."

"Do you know Mick that Maria promised me seven staff this morning but just you four are all that has come? It's all right for them upstairs they are not in the front line".

I have a VIP breakfast for 30 people in the York suite, you will have to do it on your own Mick."

"OK Rachel, I'll do it but I want to be out of here by 11.30. 1 am meeting an old friend in "Maggie's."

"Morning, I'll have an orange juice please."

"You're the guy that was looking for Dan."

"That's right, Harry's the name, and I'm meeting him here this morning."

"Should be here by now, oh look here they are now."

"Good morning, you must be Harry, come and sit over here, where we can talk privately, I'm Dan."

"I believe you know Mick, he will be in a minute."

"Top man Mick, I did a few parties last Christmas with him."

"The way I heard it was he did the work and you did the talking to the punters."

"Don't be like that, anyway I have a plan to set up a new catering agency and I am looking for your help. I have done my homework and have got about 10 waitresses I can call on. I have got a few places lined up. I was thinking about "The River Gate Hotel.""

"The Black and White Agency sends the staff to "The Gate.""

"I know that Dan, but a little bird told me they are not happy with the Black and White. If "The Gate" change to my Agency you and you team can still work here, I will pay after each day and £1 an hour more."

"Leave it with me I will talk it over with the rest of the team, I will get back to you tonight. Mum's the word okay."

"Let's go join the others in the corner Harry."

"Hi everybody, this is Harry, an old friend of yours I believe Mick."

"Hello Harry, how are you, bit out of your way out here."

Nice to see you Mick, I must rush off now people to see, places to go, hear from you later Dan."

"See you tonight Harry."

"Mick I am going back at 12.15pm I want to have a chat with Darren, the Banqueting Manager, about his staff problems."

"The word is Harry is going out on his own Dan, remember make sure any of his promises are up front, I mean money."

"Thanks Mick, I will remember that."

"He is an excellent front man Dan, but very selfish."

"Hiya Jackie, how are you, been lucky lately?"

"I have been out of town doing Relief Head Waiter for a few weeks at The Durham Restaurant". Have you been there Dan?"

"I can't remember, maybe, must go Jackie, see you later."

"Darren have you got a couple of minutes."

"Sure Dan, come into my office. Coffee?"

"Two sugars, thanks Darren."

"I am hoping we can do some business together."

"Go on, Dan, how?"

"How if you brought another agency in and certain top-class waiters and waitresses came with it?"

"But we use the Black and White for our banquets, that's top management decision Dan."

"I understand there is going to be a new management team shortly so, a new brush brushes clean, know what I mean Darren?"

"But where does that leave you and your team? If the Black and White goes."

"Maybe I might work for the new agency you never know Darren."

"I will give it a lot of thought Dan."

"When does the new manager start?"

"First Monday in September. I'll let you know probably on the Tuesday."

"Thanks Darren, see you later."

"Martin I have just been upstairs with Darren the banqueting manager. I have been giving it a bit of thought for some time now about working for him on banquets and conferences."

"But Dan, Maria sends all the staff here and she wouldn't do it, she has an unwritten contract."

"Listen Martin, what if another agency turns up, charges less."

"You don't mean Harry do you? That's why he wanted to talk to you. What's his plan?"

"Not his plan Martin, mine. Every one of us is capable of running a function or wedding. We are all top table executive waiters with exception of one or two. What are we doing carrying big trays, doing breakfasts? We should be in bed at 7.00am not working."

"I get Harry in, Maria's staff are out, that includes us. He has about 10 staff of his own. All we do is change sides but this time he sends his staff to "The Anchor Restaurant" and we go downstairs to the banqueting department. We still get paid after each shift here and Harry sends his invoice in and collects his fee for staff supplied."

"What about Maria?"

"What about Maria? Where is she going to send all the spare staff, we will have to take work where we can get it, like here for example, it is not our fault, she sends about seven good staff and 10 rubbish ones. Rachel books six she gets four. Us! Have you seen some of the staff she sent for Darren? I liked working with them sometimes, they made me look brilliant!"

"Dan, I'll keep it under my hat at the moment, keep me posted."

"Let's get this section cleared and set up for dinner. To tell you the truth I will be pleased to be away from these tours, they are pushed about like sheep. They arrive at 5.00pm, dinner at 7.00pm, bed at 10pm, breakfast at 7.00am and gone on the coach at 9.00am, to do it all again in Edinburgh. They don't see outside of hotels from stepping off the plane in London."

"I'm going straight home after lunch, do you want a lift today Dan?"

"Sure Martin, I am doing a private dinner for Maria tonight, I want to be sober."

"Hello is Harry there please? Tell him it's Dan"

 "Hello Dan, I was just having a sandwich. Any news?"

"Harry, I might be able to get you in at "The River Gate" but it will cost you."

"How much Dan? I'm only a poor waiter."

"Bollocks Harry, there is no such thing as a poor waiter, £250 up front, cash no cheques and £250 after you have been in one month."

"Wa'aat, that's a monkey, £500. Where would I get that?"

"Harry I must go now, if you can't get the cash, forget it, ring me tomorrow, bye."

"Hi Joan, I bet you the phone rings in about five minutes."

"What makes you so sure he'll go for it Dan?"

"He is greedy Joan, he knows if he gets in "The Gate" he will make a fortune. Every time Maria sends me for a five hour shift on breakfast she charges £2 per hour, that's £10 so if she sends five staff that's £50, five days £250, that's £1,000 per month and that's only five of us. At this moment Harry will have his calculator out counting how much he is going to make."

"There you are Dan, it's ringing."

"Let it ring Joan, let him wait."

"Hello, Dan here."

"Harry here, Dan I have thought about what you said, when do you want the first £250."

"Tuesday 2nd September in my hand, that's when you maybe in at "The Gate, remember it is just maybe, but have the money ready anyway okay? See you later."

"See you then Dan, bye."

"Good morning everyone, I'm sure you are all surprised to see me on breakfast, not that Rachel is not doing a marvellous job, it is that today sees the arrival of Mr Tropez our new General Manager, he comes very highly thought of by Head Office."

"Where is Pedro, Pablo?"

"I have let him have a lie in today, poor dear, he was up all night hanging wallpaper in our lounge, Mick, he will be on at lunch."

"Do you think there will be many changes Pablo?"

"I would think so Chris, but not in this department, we have turned round, don't you think."

"I like the way you include us Pablo, it is not often we get any credit for anything."

"Mr Tropez has arranged a meeting with all heads of departments together and then individually tomorrow morning."

"Can we get on with checking these breakfast tables Pablo, the tours will be in soon."

"Sorry Mick, just thought I would let you know about the new manager."

"Rachel how many staff have you booked from the agency for breakfast."

"I told her six but it's just the usual four turns up, Pablo."

"It has been happening a lot lately Rachel. We may have to take a look at other agencies."

"Did you hear that Dan, Pablo's timing could not have been better?"

"Perfect. I hope he mentions it to Mr Tropez I know Darren will. Things may be looking up."

"I have not had a lot to do with Darren, Dan what type of guy is he? He seems to know what he is doing."

"He sure knows what he is doing, first and foremost he has come through the ranks. He was trained in London and if you look at him you can see he is a waiter, very smart and he has style, and a nice bloke. He is married with two young boys and a wife who gives him a hard time."

"I think you better put the rest of the team in the picture about Maria getting blown out Dan."

"I will this morning in "Maggie's" I am going to phone Harry to come and explain his point of view to the rest."

"Where is Harry then Dan?"

"He'll be here Chris, he'll be here."

"What's it all about Mick? Who's this guy Harry then?"

Here he is now, Billy, all will be revealed."

"My name is Harry and I have a small agency and I am expanding, through the grapevine I have heard that for me to succeed I need the best and that is why I am here. I am willing to pay £1 per hour more than you are getting now and can guarantee you plenty of work."

"Hold it Harry, my name is Billy. I also speak for Jean here but we have all the work we need at "The Gate" from Maria's agency."

"I was just getting to that, as you know there is a new General Manager and my spies tell me as from tomorrow Maria will be out and all staff will come from me."

"I have about 10 and Jackie phoned me last night."

"Was he sober Harry?"

"That was uncalled for Chris, even half-cut Jackie is as good as some staff I know, present company excluded."

"What do you think Mick? you have worked with Harry here, and will he deliver?"

"I hope so, I am staying here I don't care whose agency as long as I get paid."

"There is one more thing - your boss from now on will be Darren from banqueting, and I will be sending my waitresses to Pablo."

"You mean banquets and weddings? I like it. No more early mornings. I'm up for it."

"I was hoping you would be Dan, there will be plenty of top table jobs for you. Will your wife come too?"

"You will have to ask her yourself Harry nobody speaks for Joan, only Joan."

"I want to speak to her anyway, I will ring her. I have a nice little job for her in Halifax, I will ask everybody not to say anything to anyone about our conversation until its official."

"Harry, will you give me a lift back home this afternoon, we have some things to discuss."

"Dan will be my right hand man at "The Gate" so if you have any problems see him."

"Do you always drive so fast Harry, Harry try and keep both hands on the wheel. Have you got my cash?"

"It's in the dashboard Dan, sorry there is only £200."

"Don't worry Harry, that's £300 you owe me next month, let's hope things work out, I have put my reputation on the line."

"Don't worry I won't let you down."

CHAPTER 7
DEREK CROOK

"Dan, could I have a word in private?"

"Sure Mick, let's go over to the table."

"Do you know anything about the "Grand Hotel", just outside Leeds?"

"Sure, it is four star and has a good restaurant, why?"

"I spoke to Maria the other night and she said she had two weeks work for me at £250 per week as head waiter while their head waiter is on holiday, so I am going to take it."

Who's the restaurant manager, do you know?"

"Oh I know alright, but I was sworn to secrecy, but I can tell you it's Derek Crook."

"Whaaat, I thought he was dead or in jail! I have often wondered where he was. I have never known anyone like him. He is probably the most professional headwaiter I have ever known. Always immaculate, style, class, he has the lot. I knew him before he started wearing wigs. I remember him telling me it was you Dan who introduced him to special brew."

"Where did you work with him Mick?"

"It was Scarborough, about 15 years ago, he had just started wearing wigs. I have never known anyone like him, very selfish with three weaknesses, money, special brew and women, any women." "Do you know I have never met anyone who hadn't got a lot of respect for him Mick? I wish you all the best. When do you go?"

"Monday. Dan, I'll see you Friday anyway."

Mick arrived about 10.30 am at the reception.

"Good morning, I am here to see Mr. Crook, my name is Mick Doyle."

"He is expecting you, just go through to the restaurant."

"Hello Mick, long time, no see. You seem to have put a few pounds around the waist."

"Nice to see you again Derek. Been here long?"

"About two years Mick, the management don't know much, which makes my job easier."

"You don't change much Derek, do you?"

"Come, we will have a coffee and I will show you where to put your stuff, have you got your evening suit with you?"

"Of course, I am a head waiter Derek.

"Have you seen anything of Dan and Martin? the last time I heard of them they were at "Monk's."

"So was I Derek, I'll tell you all about it sometime."

"The word I heard Dan was a very naughty Monk and he was called Rasputin."

"He certainly was a naughty Monk Derek, but he has changed a lot, doesn't drink now, married with a son."

"Doesn't drink Dan, doesn't drink, how does he do this job and not drink, he was the one who introduced me to special brew lager, how long has he been stopped?"

"A few years ago now Derek, I'll tell him you are still drinking them."

"Now Mick, I have a good system going here, this will be a good earner for you, as long as you don't get greedy."

We do a lot of chance trade in this restaurant, a lot of parties of eight upwards. That's where you come in."

"What about the booze Derek."

"I keep a stock of Carlsberg under my desk, you can help yourself, but leave some for me."

"This is how it works Mick, I take the order, I give the top copy to the chef, the middle copy goes to the cashier and I keep the bottom copy. When the customer asks for his bill I will go in the kitchen and retrieve the chef's copy without him seeing, under the pretence of looking at the order."

"But what about the cashier Derek?"

"Don't worry about her, we have an arrangement."

"You mean she is in on it?"

"Well let's put it this way, she is very fond of me."

"You have it all tied up haven't you?"

"I do my best Mick, I do my best," laughed Derek, admiring his new blonde wig in the mirror.

I will pass you the bill, you bring it to the host of the party, making sure on two points. 1. The credit card machine is broke, 2. You don't let him take the bill with him. This makes the party disappear, no evidence of even being there."

"What then?"

"Take the bill and money straight to me in the gents where we split 50-50, and don't bring the receipt back to the customer, I will take over from there,"

After a few days Mick phoned Dan.

"Dan, I need a bit of advice here, Derek is ripping the bills off. I am no saint, but he wants to hit three bills a night. I don't mind one for my petrol and rent, but he is over the top. He has this young girl as a cashier, she's about 22, totally infatuated by him, and he gives her about £2 out of a £40 bill, stingy bastard."

"Of course you knew what he was like Mick, if anything goes wrong he won't get his hands burnt."

"But wait until you hear the best part. Jenny the cashier has just told him she is pregnant and he wants me to hit a big bill on Saturday to pay for a termination."

"Is Derek the father?"

"No, it turns out its some well-known celebrity, who was staying in the hotel and Derek does not want to lose his partner in crime."

"Tell him to piss off Mick and get out of there, phone Maria and tell her you have broken your ankle or something, if it goes wrong you will be the fall guy."

"OK Dan, I'll work until Friday then phone up and go to "The Gate" with you lot instead."

Mick worked until Friday, phoned Maria and Maria phoned Derek. She phoned Derek at home.

"Mick, I hope your ankle gets better. Mr. Crook was very upset, I will have to find someone else for him."

"Thanks Maria, hope to see you soon."

Mick thought to himself, "I am sure Derek is upset, but not about me, about having to pay for Jenny's bother himself."

When Mick turned up at "Maggie's" Friday night, Martin met him with a smile on his face.

"How did you get on with Derek Crook, Mick?"

"He is well named Martin, Crook by name and crook by nature. I have never worked with such a stingy bastard, and I hope not to again."

CHAPTER 8
THE TIP BOX

"Hi Martin, its Maria here, fancy some work?" "I could do with a couple of hours work Maria, Brenda, the wife, has gone to her sisters for a couple of weeks to give me a rest, since her stroke I have had to do everything for her and Nathan has moved in with his girlfriend, said Martin.

"I need about five staff all in, and I can't seem to catch Dan or Joan in. They are probably doing their own thing now that Joan has a car. I think Mick has teamed up with that Harry, I understand he is trying to start an agency and poach all my good staff Martin?"

"I have not heard anything about any agency or Mick's whereabouts, maybe he is on a bender" lied Martin. "I will call up to his flat and get back to you. Anyway Maria what's this job you got?"

"There's a new Restaurant opening next Tuesday above the old Barclays Bank in town, the owner is a friend of mine and he has been let down by his Restaurant Manager and four staff who have to give one months' notice in their present job. It will probably be about three weeks work. Try and get back to me as soon as you can Martin, Can I count on you?"

"Sure Maria I should be able to get a team together, ring you later" assured Martin. He knew Dan and Joan were with Mick doing some jobs for Harry, but he did not want to tell Maria because he knew they would need her again. Martin rang Harry on his mobile.

"Hi, that you Harry, its Martin here, could you ask Mick to give me a ring".

"We're busy here at the moment Martin I have a marquee job on, I will ask him to ring you when it gets a bit quiet. I could have done with you and Nathan here today" said an excited Harry.

That night Mick rang Martin,

"Martin, sorry I did not get back to you but I was having a few glasses of happiness after the job"

"Mick, I got a call from Maria. She has got a magic job for a couple of weeks in town, she said she had been trying to get in touch with you, I said you were probably on a bender, she has also been trying to ring Dan and Joan, I said I had no idea. She mentioned Harry, I pretended I knew nothing. Anyway next Tuesday. I will get back with details later, I will ring Dan and Joan at home, and it will be good working with you again. By the way Chris is also included - you tell him to ring Maria. See you."

"Is that Martin, Dan here, Mick has just phoned. Count Joan and me in. I will ring Maria, I will tell her we have been on holidays. See you later, I am going to a meeting."

Maria rang Martin on Friday.

"Martin, will you call in and have a talk with Philip Brown the owner of the new Restaurant "Windows".

"Okay Maria. Did the others get in touch?"

"Yes thanks Martin, must go bye." said Maria.

"Hello, you must be Martin, I'm Philip Brown the Proprietor" announced this tall casually dressed, well-tanned, gentleman about 35. Come over to the bar and we can have a chat"

Martin thought to himself 'This is a man with class' and followed him across to the bar.

"I have spent a lot of money converting this floor into a Restaurant and you may have noticed why it's called "Windows" began Philip. Martin thought it was a good name as there were large windows on each of the three sides and above the kitchen, a large mirror.

"I am opening Tuesday next week. You will be in complete control. I have some staff of my own, Maria tells me your team are top class, and there will always be plenty of work here if things take off."

"I must interrupt you Philip, can I call you Philip? But I will only be able to help you for a couple of weeks until your new man gets here, I have a poorly wife at home so I can't take anything permanent.'

"I will be quite honest with you Martin you have got me out of the shit and I will be very grateful over and above what the agency is paying you. Anyway come and I will show you around."

The room was large with a high ceiling. There were some beautiful pictures of abstract art around the room, with a large chandelier in the middle. The chairs and table legs were all carved in flower design. There were ice buckets at each table. The table cloths were white with royal blue slip cloths. The kitchen was having the final touches, joiners and plumbers were hard at work.

"I think we will go now and let the workmen finish off" said Philip.

"You have a very modern and upmarket Restaurant there Philip. I must get off now, see you Tuesday." said Martin as he made for the stairs.

"Are we all here now" announced Martin.

"Just Mick to come, he has an appointment at his office at 10.30 "said Chris - laughing.

When Mick arrived Martin produced a large tip box and placed it in the corner near the window. Service began at 12.30 and lunch finished at 2.30.

"I think this is going to be a good little earner Martin" said Mick "I have put eight pounds in the tip box."

Martin began putting his famous 10% discretional service charge on bills over six people. After a few days they shared the tips and each received about thirty pounds. On Saturday morning Dan exclaimed.

"Anybody moved the tip box? It's gone!"

"What" Mick rushed across to the table where the box had been" I don't believe it, is this a wind up, there must have been about £150 00 in it"

"It was under the table when we left last night I put it there myself" said Martin.

"I am going down to speak to the security guy he would surely remember anybody carrying a box that size" said Dan.

"Have you got a video of the staff leaving here last week Bill" Dan said to the head security man in his office.

"Sure have Dan have a look yourself" and proceeded to play last night's video.

"The last man to leave was the chef Dan and as you can see he was carrying nothing" said Bill.

Dan went back upstairs and reported back to the team. The other staff were just young and above suspicion.

"This puts us all in the frame Martin" said Chris.

Work carried on through lunch and Dan brought another box that evening for dinner. It was a busy night as usual about £100.00 in tips including the 10% service charge. The Restaurant closed as usual and everyone left, leaving the box safely under the table out of sight and Dan had the key.

"See you Monday" shouted Dan as he headed home with Joan. Joan gave the baby sitter a lift home she said to Dan "You saw the video of everyone leaving Friday night right? I have been giving this a lot of thought, the Restaurant is closed tomorrow but we will go early on Monday Morning "announced Joan.

"I have an idea and I am surprised you smart waiters did not think of it."

"Nobody went out the door with the box did they?" "You think it is still there" said Dan.

"I will show you Monday" laughed Joan.

On Monday morning Joan and Dan headed off at 8.30am, instead of 10.30am .They parked the car opposite the Restaurant and sat back to wait to see who went in.

"I bet you that chef is first to arrive this morning" said Joan.

"What makes you think that?" asked Dan.

"Just wait and see" answered Joan." here he comes now."

"Bloody hell Joan, how did you know that, and there is his second chef Tom as well".

"That Tom won't go in, he will walk around the side and when he does, so will we, and I bet you we will find our tip box is there as well." said Joan" Give the head chef five minutes to get in."

When Joan and Dan walked around the comer there was the tip box being lowered down by a long chord into the arms of Tom.

"Morning Tom, you're early today I think you better shout up to your mate to haul the box back up again don't you" snapped Dan. With that Tom dropped the box and ran like hell.

Dan picked up the box and carried it around the front just in time to see the head chef vanish around the other corner. When Martin arrived and heard the story he said, "I suppose I better phone Maria for a couple of chefs, I have a feeling we are going to be short in the kitchen this lunchtime."

"I think we should share the tips after each meal in future starting after lunch and I vote Joan gets £5.00 off each of us for her brilliant detective work." said Mick.

"I'll second that" said Chris.

"Clever swine that cook coming in early, I think that is the first time I have heard of chef ripping off waiters".

The team worked one more week until Mr Cortez and his team arrived. Martin told him the story of Chef Jones, if that was his real name and they both had a good laugh.

CHAPTER 9
GYPSY WEDDING

Darren phoned Dan

"Wait till you see the two dolly birds I have starting tonight Dan, I have a good team now and Jack and Harry don't have a job now, see you tonight"

"Do I know them Darren?" Asked Dan

"No I don't think so, they are originally from Manchester" replied Darren. Dan had not worked in Manchester.

Joan and Dan were a bit late arriving for the banquet. The rest were there and Dan noticed Billy and Jean were back from Spain with nice tans.

"Hi Amigos" shouted Dan. "Nice to have you back in the fold." Billy and Jean waved.

"I want you to meet Jan and Jill" announced Darren. Dan turned around to see two quite attractive girls, about 30, standing there.

"Hi, I'm Jan and this is Jill, Darren's told us about you Dan hope we meet with your approval?"

"Hi I'm Dan's wife Joan, if you come with me I'll show you what's to be done." With that she ushered the two girls into the kitchen, smiling at Dan as she walked past, Joan knew both Jill and Jan were Dan's handwriting.

Dan was on the top table as usual. Joan took the two girls under her wing and he noticed they were quite good and pleasant to the guests and he thought, "Darren seems to have got it right this time compared with some of the other staff he hired".

The meal finished early enough for the staff to call at "Maggie's". Harry and Jack seemed to be discussing business in the corner. It broke their hearts to get blown out at "The Gate" and having to work as waiters like everyone else queuing up for their cash.

Everyone seemed to be there that night. Mick, Chris, Martin, Nathan, Billy, Jean, Brian, Susan, Joan, Dan and now Jill and Jan.

"Hi, you lot, shouted Jack, "I need three staff for a wedding next Saturday, how about you Chris? I need someone to take charge?"

"I want to be paid on Saturday before I leave, Jack," said Chris.

"OK Chris, what about the two new girls?"

Jan looked at Jill and they both nodded.

"Cash on Saturday? Okay" said Jill "give us the details tomorrow night at "The Gate."

On Saturday Chris got to the "Windsor" early and went straight to the reception desk.

"Good morning my name is Chris, I am from the agency, I am the head waiter for your wedding today."

"Oh yes the Gypsy Wedding" came the reply from the receptionist.

"Sorry? Gypsy Wedding, what gypsy wedding?" said a shocked Chris.

"In the ballroom," she answered "they are in there now getting ready."

Chris immediately hurried through to the ballroom. There were some people unloading boxes of spirits and putting them on the tables.

"Good morning, I'm Chris your head waiter for the day have you got a table plan."

"I'm Joseph O'Toole" announced the older person in the room. "I have some cards for the Top Table, I would like ten round tables on each side of the dance floor.

We put bottles of spirits on each table but these are not touched, they are just a status thing."

Chris stood there gob-smacked for a few seconds turned and went back to the reception desk.

"Could I speak to the Duty Manager please?"

"Hello, I'm Mr Wilks, Duty Manager," announced the little guy "can I help you?"

"Can you tell me what is going on in the ballroom?" said an irate Chris.

"Two weeks ago two men walked up to the reception desk asked to book the ballroom for a day asked how much would a meal for 250 people and the hire of a band. They asked if they could bring their own booze, they would pay corkage.

When the then Duty Manager who has since left said it would be okay one of the men produced a bag of cash paid three grand got a receipt and walked out. It was only last week we found out it was to be a wedding. That is when we phoned Harry Smith, We know no more than that. I have a menu, standard, soup, chicken, fruit salad and coffee." said Mr Wilks.

"What about the cake?" Said Chris "There is no cake, you better ask Mr O'Toole"

Chris went back to Mr O'Toole asked him about the cake and what time the bride and groom would arrive. Mr O'Toole looked at him a bit blank.

"Oh there won't be a cake, we do things a bit different and the wedding party will be arriving around three or maybe four, we are off to meet the boat now" said Mr. O'Toole.

The staff arrived shortly after that and Chris got them altogether for a briefing.

"Welcome everyone and especially Jan and Jill from across the Pennines, we are going to have a different type of wedding today, so if you have any concerns during the meal come and see me. This is Betty the head waitress here, she has got the menu and she will give you your stations and how the tables are to be set." With that he headed off to the bar.

All the guests arrived around four and made straight for the bar. There was no one dressed as a bride or groom. When they came into the ballroom all the young men sat on one side and the girls opposite and on the top table were the older folk. Most of the men did not bother with food, and Chris noticed Jan and Jill were getting very friendly and accepting drinks from some of the young guys. The band started playing during the meal all the girls got up and danced with each other. The meal was a shambles, the chef was going crazy in the kitchen and the waitresses were getting very upset and Chris called Betty aside.

"Betty, get everything except their booze off the tables and let's get this over and we can get out of here."

"OK Chris, but there is something you must know, those two waitresses Jan and Jill are doing tricks with a lot of those young guys in the gents." said Betty.

"Whaat!" Chris hurried around to the gents there were about 12 guys hanging around outside the toilet. Chris walked straight in and was greeted with.

"Got your tenner Chris". There was Jan sitting on the sink knickers down legs up in the air with a young guy banging away. Jan had a handful of tenner's. Jill was in a cubicle with her bare arse sticking out and about four guys standing in a queue with money in their hands and one of them getting ready to mount.

"You can have a free go Chris get in the queue." Shouted Jill laughing.

Chris turned and ran out. He was white the blood had drained from his face. He made a beeline straight to the manager.

"Your gents toilets are blocked you had better sort it out now."

Just then Jack arrived to pay the staff as promised he handed Chris £30 and asked. "Did Jan and Jill come?" asked Jack.

"Oh they came alright Jack as a matter of fact they are probably still coming" exclaimed Chris.

"I'm off Jack, this was a disaster, never take another booking for a Gypsy Wedding again." said Chris.

"Why's that Chris?" asked Jack.

"Go and ask Jan and Jill they are round at the toilets, see you." With that Chris hurried off to the bar next door.

He rang Darren at "The Gate", "I think you will be two down tonight for dinner Jan and Jill" said Chris.

"What's the matter, are they too tired after the wedding." asked Darren.

"Something like that" said Chris.

Jack phoned Chris that night.

"Sorry about that job this afternoon Chris. I has no idea it was to be a Gypsy Wedding. I spoke to Mr O'Toole and he gave me £20 to give to you for the good job you done. As regards Jan and Jill I could not speak to them as they were too pissed, I will see them at "The Gate" on Monday, they will not work for me or Harry again but I can't say what Darren will do at "The Gate."

"I was quite upset at the time, the guests were all young, 20 to 25 and the more booze they got they began arguing among themselves. All the women stuck to one side and I did not even know who the bride and groom was, they just referred to the get together as the wedding season. As regards Jan and Jill I see the funny side now but when I walked into the gents I nearly died of shock."

"Thanks Chris I did not pay the girls and won't be so I will give you their money when I see you." said Jack. "Anyway Chris I have a nice little earner for you and Mick next week, lunch and dinner for two weeks at the "Saxon Hotel" in town, it's quiet at "The Gate" anyway. I have spoken to Mick and he will see you there. Monday morning at 10.30am."

"Okay, see you when I see you Jack." said Chris. It would be nice to work with his best mate Mick again. He was not too keen on seeing Jan and Jill again so soon anyway.

When Chris arrived at "The Saxon", Mick was already there. He had a big smile on his face having heard about Jan and Jill, but he had something more important to smile about.

"Good to see you Chris, have you recovered from Saturday?" laughed Mick, "let's have a coffee before the Restaurant Manager gets here."

They went into the staff hall got a couple of coffees and sat down at a table. They talked about Saturday's wedding and the two girls and then made their way down to the restaurant.

"Good morning, you must be from the Agency" announced the

supervisor," come over and meet Mr Best," they walked over to a table in the corner where a man was sitting having breakfast. "This is Mr Best," he turned round and Mick nearly collapsed.

"Mr Best, my arse, this is Derek Crook, thought a stunned Mick. It took about ten seconds to compose himself.

"Pleased to meet you Mr Best," he stuttered, the hair was dyed, the glasses, the little goatee beard but still Derek Crook. "This is Chris and my name is Mick. Pleased to meet you." The supervisor went back to work and Mr Best said with a grin.

"How are you Mick? Been a long time."

"You know each other?" asked Chris.

"Meet Derek Crook" said Mick

"The Derek Crook? Asked Chris

"The one and only" answered Mick.

"It would be highly appreciated if you called me "Mr Best." Same rules apply Mick, same days off same split, you split yours, with Chris," Mick smiled 'same old Derek' he thought.

"How long you been here Derek?" said Mick.

"About six months. This is a good little earner. The management are young and naive, they do what they are told, I have had to get rid of some staff thieving, you know, not from the hotel but from me, I caught one hitting a bill" smiled Derek. Mick and Chris burst out laughing.

"I specifically asked Harry for you and Chris." Harry or Jack did not tell Mick.

"How are you Chris? I have not had the pleasure" shaking Chris's hand.

"Count your fingers Chris" laughed Mick.

Mick began looking around "There is somebody missing Derek where is she?"

"Natalie darling, come and meet an old friend of ours." shouted Derek.

Just then this attractive brunette walked towards him.

"Hi Mick" she announced to a stunned Mick "recovered from your drink problem? Welcome aboard."

"Jenny, I knew you had to be here somewhere, nice to see you, you look marvellous, like the brunette look." smiled Mick.

This restaurant was not as busy as "The Windsor" so more caution was needed. Derek still collected the top copy from the chef's spike but Mick told Chris he has to keep a keen eye on the chef. He didn't drink.

"Not as busy as the last place Derek" said Mick.

"Busy enough" muttered Derek.

In the first week Mick hit about ten bills amounting to about three hundred and fifty pounds.

"Here Chris," he gave Chris fifty pounds.

"Thanks Mick, but you better be careful I was watching that chef the other day, I might be wrong but he seemed to be counting his top copies a couple of times with a frown on his forehead." said Chris.

"Okay, I'll tell Derek." said Mick "he seems to be getting very reckless since I first worked with him, I will be careful."

It was important that Mick kept his distance from Derek and always referred to him as Mr Best, but being the professional as he was he did it well. He trusted Chris, they were close.

Sunday lunch was very busy.

"We will do well today Mick. Do you want a couple of "carlies" to keep up your speed." said Derek.

He had about a dozen in an ice-box under his desk.

"Thanks Derek, give me a couple for Chris as well." said Mick. They nipped out the back and quickly polished them off.

"There is something not right here" said Chris "I am going back to "The Gate" next week, Derek is taking too many chances Mick we are all going to end up in deep shit. Remember the agency is involved. Derek is very selfish, he is always pissing about with that cashier, and she is obsessed with him."

"After lunch today I'll phone Harry and tell him were going back to "The

Gate" then" agreed Mick, he always trusted Chris.

"Sorry Derek but I have to send Mick and Chris to another job at the club or I will lose my money" lied Harry on the phone.

"Don't send me anybody else then" shouted Derek sounding pissed.

I think he is pissed up Mick," said Harry.

"I know he is, he is a lot worse than he was." said Mick as he headed off to "Maggie's".

About a fortnight later Mick phoned Chris.

"I owe you one Chris, you won't guess what has happened to Mr Best."

"Go on then Mick tell me."

"Tell you tonight in "Maggie's" replied Mick.

After work the whole team are having a few dozen winding down glasses in "Maggie's" when Mick comes in from "The Gate".

"Go on then Mick tells us about Mr Best."

"Remember that busy Sunday lunch, well the next one was busier and since Derek had no one he could trust he started doing the double getting both copies and presenting the bills himself, after the lunch he was heading to his car, briefcase and umbrella when this guy shouted, could we have a word Mr Best." Derek recognised two customers from the lunch.

"Oh hello, enjoyed your lunch sir, hope to see you again," and carried on walking towards his car.

The lady and gentleman came across to him.

"Excellent lunch Mr Best, excellent service, now could we have a look in your briefcase," at the same time flashing a police warrant card. When they opened a shocked Derek's briefcase they found a bundle of notes, opening the bundle they ran a light over each note and a blue stain showed up."

"Do you always take the hotels money home with you Mr Best?"

"I have no idea what you are talking about" said Derek as he was officially arrested "It only turned out he had been at it from day one. They planted about twelve tables of two police officers and marked the money and the greedy bastard broke his own rules of hitting nothing less than a four table. He hit seven two's himself. If they had decided to do that two weeks ago he would have had us implicated."

"It looks like Mr Best is not the best after all, wait till they find out his real name is Mr Derek Crook ha ha. "laughed Chris. Mick just whispered to Dan "But for the Grace of God."

Months later Martin phoned Mick.

"Mick, your pal Derek and his lady accomplice got themselves some porridge Derek got 18 months and Jenny 3 months. It was their third offence. Word is he is restaurant manager in the Officer's Mess in Leeds Jail"

"Serves him right, selfish swine" replied Mick smiling. "Although I do feel a bit sorry for Jenny, she was only carrying out Derek's orders, I have no doubt they will turn up somewhere else in a couple of years."

CHAPTER 10
THE SALES CONFERENCE

"Hi Dan, Darren here. There is not a lot of work next week but a mate of mine in Manchester has got a sales conference and he desperately needs staff."

"Darren, why don't you ring Harry?" asked Dan

"He doesn't want to pay a fee to the agency Dan, he just wants six staff, stay overnight if you want, I will even go myself," replied Darren.

That night in "Maggie's", Dan was looking for volunteers to go to the job on Saturday.

"Jan and I will go," shouted Jill across to Dan.

"Okay but you two will have to behave yourselves," answered Dan laughing.

"We'll go said Billy and Jean, "we need the money."

When Dan and Darren arrived at the "Palace Hotel" they met Charles, the manager and he explained that the dinner that night was for 100 salesmen and that there would be a blue comedian and two strippers, so the dinner had to be over by 9.30pm. Billy and Jean arrived with Jan and Jill and Charles showed them to their rooms.

They all met downstairs in the staff bar later.

"I hope you girls behave yourselves tonight, we want to be out of there by half nine, there is a comedian and two strippers on after the meal," announced Dan. "I don't suppose you want to stay and watch the cabaret, you two will probably be going up the town, clubbing."

"You'd better believe we will," laughed Jan.

Charles had five of his own staff, the rest had flu. Charles also forgot to tell Darren that the sales conference had been in for two days and they had given the staff a hard time, and that was probably the reason he had phoned Darren.

"Hi, I'm George, the head chef, you must have come with Darren. I hope you have a better time with these wallies than I've had for the past two days."

"Don't worry chef, we've had plenty of these jobs at "The Gate," said Billy.

"Is that young chef Juhuno still there, I trained him," said the chef.

"He's the main man now chef."

"Does he still lose the head when he gets too much booze? He once put a kitchen porter in the steamer and got a verbal warning. At every staff party he got drunk, got jealous and punched anyone speaking to his wife, and now he's the head chef, but I suppose he could cook. He was well trained!" laughed the chef.

When the meal got under way, Darren could see it was going to be a long drawn out affair. There was plenty of booze about and Jan and Jill had their fair share, each time they came into the kitchen. Billy and Jean worked well together. Jean was about 30, slim and very attractive. She had blond hair tied back and was about 5ft.5" tall. Billy was tall for a waiter, but had a pleasant manner with the customer's. He was always close to Jean, a bit jealous.

Dan was on the top table, as usual. People kept getting up and going to the bar during the meal, this infuriated Dan as he hated these all male sales conference dinners. Halfway through the main course, Charles came across to Darren, and they were in deep discussion.

"What was all that about Darren?" asked Dan.

"The stripper can't come, her car's been broken into and all her gear has gone and it's too late to get another one," said Darren.

"Maybe not," said Dan laughing," Why don't you ask Jan and Jill, they're game for anything, remember the gypsy wedding?"

"You must be joking, Dan," said Darren, "Charles wouldn't go for it."

"Don't tell him, go and see the girls and ask them if they are game. I will speak to the main man, explain the situation and tell him to have a whip round," explained Dan.

"Are you sure Dan?" asked Darren.

"They both have nice figures and they are always telling us that they wear stockings instead of tights, you go and see them," said Dan laughing.

Darren headed across to talk to the girls and Dan ambushed Mr Grant, the head sales director.

"Could I have a private word Mr Grant?"

"Sure Dan, everything's going well, I hope none of my staff are giving you a hard time?"

"I have a big problem I must discuss with you about your cabaret act after the meal," said Dan. He looked up to see Darren give him the thumbs up from across the room.

"Your original cabaret can't make it but I have arranged two substitutes, but you will have to organise a whip round before they perform."

"No problem Dan, just get me an empty ice bucket and I'll start the collection myself with a tenner".

When coffee was being served Darren said he would do the D.J. bit as he had done a bit at "The Gate". The equipment had been prepared during the day for the original artist.

After the meal the guests all settled down for the cabaret. The comedian came across to Darren.

"I understand there has been a change of plan. By the way, my name is Seamus O'Conner," he said in a broad Liverpool accent.

"Yes there has, but don't worry, come with me and I will introduce you to the girls"

Darren brought Seamus round to the bar.

"Hi Jill, who's you friend?" said Seamus pointing at Jan.

"Hello Seamus, this is Jan," came the reply.

"You two know each other?" said Darren quite shocked.

"Yes Darren. I used to work with Seamus in the Working Men's Clubs a few years ago."

"You're not too bothered about this gig tonight then?"

"Not as long as I'm paid well and don't worry about Jan, we will give them their money's worth tonight!"

"That's what I am worried about. Jill, just remember this is a four star hotel and Charles the manager is a friend of mine."

The comedian was quite good but Dan could see that the guests were more interested in who was coming on next

The lights went down and Darren put on the strippers music (da da da daa) and up popped Jill on the stage and started her dance, then, not to be out done, Jan joined her.

"Let's give them some," whispered Jill to a very excited and willing Jan. "Slowly take off your uniform and follow me."

Jan replied, "I could really take to this, Jill."

Jill came off the stage and with willing assistance, climbed on to the first of the long tables and started to strut her stuff. Jan followed. By the time they'd got around to the top table, the delegates were ecstatic. The main man was loving it. They began making obscene gestures with the wine bottles and carried on around the u-shaped table and then returned for their finale on the stage. After a few more shakes of their now naked breasts, they turned around, touched their toes, showed their bare bums and left the stage.

"Where is my drink, Dan?" said a knackered Jill. Dan handed both girls two very large gin and tonics and two hotel dressing gowns and they hastily darted to the lift up to their rooms. The clapping and the cheering were still going on ten minutes after it was over.

"She hasn't lost her touch has she, that Jill?" said Seamus to Dan.

"I have seen it all now Seamus, true professionals, the show must go on."

Dan made a bee-line for Mr Grant who was in charge of the ice bucket.

"Thanks a lot Dan, you've done us proud. Here's the money for the girls and here's a little something for your help," said Mr Grant.

"Glad to be of help, thanks, I must be off now," and with that Dan slipped the £20 into his pocket, took the ice bucket and headed off to see the girls upstairs.

"Girls, its Dan here. I have brought you your money, I'm coming in, and I hope you are dressed." With that he went in to find the two girls tearing into a bottle of gin.

"There is nearly £300 here Jill, of course there would have to be my negotiating fee out of that, 10% okay?"

"Okay Dan, do you want a drink?"

"No thanks, don't drink but I wouldn't mind a ....."

"Piss off Dan, see you in the morning"

The next morning everyone headed home. Jean would not go in the same car as Jan and Jill.

"I'm not travelling with those two slags," announced Jean. So both Billy and Jean returned with Darren and Dan after what Darren referred to as a 'job well done'.

When Jan and Jill got back to their flat they poured themselves a drink and sat down to relax after the journey.

"Well, what did you think Jan?" asked Jill," enjoy it?"

"It was an experience Jill, some of those guys were trying to touch me but I must admit I would not have done it if I was sober," laughed Jan. "I think I will stick to waiting on tables rather than dancing on them, I nearly fell off twice."

Jan and Jill had been friends since school days. They'd worked as waitresses or barmaids around the country, in the summer at the seaside and in the winter in the city. Jill was of mixed race, 5ft 6", was pretty and had been married twice. Her second husband, the father of their two children, just upped and went back to St Kitts with the kids. He'd said he did not want his kids to live in England. When Jill had too much to drink she'd sometimes become very depressed. She always phoned them every week and began saving her money to go and visit them.

"I will put this unexpected wind-fall in the bank towards my trip to see my Leroy and Sharon next summer, Jan."

"We could go with a job like this every week Jill," said Jan laughing. She had her own problems with men, she was always falling in love and was devastated when her husband ran off with her sister. She fancied Dan, but Dan was in love with Joan.

"Do you think I might one day have a chance with Dan?" said Jan.

"Maybe, he is a very genuine bloke, good at his job and doesn't drink. I think he is wasted on that Joan. I like her, but she is always trying to do him down."

"Mick told me he used to drink a lot and lost many jobs due to booze, I could not imagine him pissed up," said Jill, "anyway, maybe Joan will up and off and you will get your chance."

"Some chance of that Jill," said Jan and they then decided to go down to the supermarket.

CHAPTER 11

BRADFORD BILL TRAP

During the weekly pool game at "Maggie's", the talk was about the forthcoming work situation. The "River Gate" had decided to decorate and close the main restaurant for about three works.

"What are we going to do for the next few weeks?" said Chris.

"Don't worry Chris something will crop up, it always does? There must be some struggling manager out there who could do with our professional skills," laughed Mick.

"It suits me fine, I have got some decorating of my own to do and then I am going to take our James to Butlins for a week," said Joan.

"Is Dan going, Joan?" asked Mick.

"No chance. That's one of the reasons I'm going with our James, to get a rest from him!" laughed Joan.

"We know where there's plenty of work, don't we Jean," shouted Billy from the bar.

"Where is that Billy?" asked Mick.

"Bradford, the "Park Court", we have just left. Harry sent us last week. Harry does not know yet but I am going to give him a ring after I have a drink."

The door opened and Martin and Dan came in. Mick shouted over.

"Martin, did you know "The "Gate" will be closed for a few weeks starting next Monday?"

"Yeah, we know Mick. It's not as if it doesn't need it, it's getting a bit scruffy. We will have to give Harry a ring. I know there is no work from the "Black and White.""

"I think you should have a talk with Billy and Jean, they're over in the corner."

"Dan, you have a word with Billy, I need a pint, you want a coke?"

"Okay Martin, put ice in it and a piece of lemon," said Dan as he made his way across to Billy and Jean.

"Go on then Billy, tell us what's happened."

"Tell him Billy, tell him," said Jean

"Harry sent us to the "Park Court" for what he said would be a nice little earner with plenty of tips," said Billy

"You should have known Billy that Harry would only be interested in his fee," said Dan.

"Oh there were plenty of tips Dan, only thing was we never got any. The restaurant was very busy, seating for about 150 with about 30 tables. 10% service charge was added to each bill and this went straight to the manager who in turn paid us it back as wages at the end of the night. Jean put £32 in tips in the box last Saturday and when she finished at 11.00pm he paid her £25. For her tips he said that the casual staff were not entitled to tips."

"So I paid myself for working and gave the manager £7 for the privilege," snapped Jean.

"What a rip off. The best of all was that he did not have any full time staff, only his two sons. Wait until I see Harry," said Billy.

"I have heard about this guy Martin, is his name Lopez, Billy?" asked Dan

"Jose Lopez, he likes to be called Mr Jose."

"Martin, why don't we go across there and teach him a lesson, it would serve him right to get some of his own medicine, we could pull the Derek Crook scam with the bills," said Mick smiling.

"It would serve him right. I had a few drinks with a few waiters and waitresses at the bar next to the "Park Court" and everyone who has been there has been ripped off. He knows we can't complain because we don't pay tax," said Billy.

"But Harry pays our tax," said Chris.

"You hope Chris, you hope,*' laughed Mick.

"Don't say anything to Harry or Jack about what we have been talking about," said Martin," the least amount of people who know what we are up to, the better. I will phone Harry and tell him we need work and hint about the "Park Court."

"When Lopez finds out we have gone he will be phoning Harry, three other girls said they will not be going back, so he is going to need about four or five staff."

Everyone drifted off home soon after. The team did not have to wait long.

"Harry, we are having our evening meal, can't it wait?" asked Joan. "Dan, phone, it's Harry, he seems desperate."

"Hi Harry, what's the matter?"

"I'm looking for a big favour Dan, and I said to the wife if anyone can help its Dan," said Harry.

"Never mind the bullshit Harry, what is it?" pretending not to know, Dan smiled across at Joan.

"I have been let down on a job and I need about five staff for a friend of mine in Bradford, it could be for a few weeks, five pounds an hour and paid at the end of each shift," pleaded Harry.

"Suits me Harry, as you know, the "River Gate" is closed for decorating and I know "Harrogate Jackie" is looking for work, I will ring him. You ring Martin, Mick and Chris. Joan can't go, she's off to Butlins with our James, for a break away from me."

"That's great Dan, I have got some from Bradford going in tonight, but I will be able to phone the manager and tell him the A-team will be there tomorrow night. Jack will be pleased, I told him he could rely on you;' said Harry.

"Hi Mick, will you pick up Chris and meet us in the "Queens Pub" next door at about 5.30pm. "Harrogate Jackie" is coming he will make his own way, he lives outside Bradford now. Martin is picking me up, see you tomorrow," said Dan.

When everyone arrived Martin got the drinks and sat down to plan the bill scam.

"Remember this guy Lopez was once a waiter, so he will be watching out for tips vanishing so make sure everything goes in the box. Chris you watch out for his sons, they are waiters. This guy Lopez has been ripping off staff and customers alike. The customer gives us £5 or £10 for the service we give them not to the manager so hopefully in the next couple of weeks we will strike a blow for waiting staff."

"You know I don't want anything to do with the knocking off the bills Martin, but I will do my best to look after the punters," said Dan.

"You have changed Dan, when you were drinking, you would not have given it a second thought," said Mick.

"That was a long time ago Mick. People change you know, when you stop drinking you will know what I mean," said Dan hopefully.

"Good evening everyone, my name is Jose Lopez, you can call me Mr Jose. I am the Maître' D. Harry has phoned me to tell me he calls you all his A-team. I just have a few rules, no drinking during service and all the tips go in the box at the desk. That's why I pay £5 per hour. I would like Martin to take the orders and present the bills. Harry said I should have no problems as I have had lots of problems with staff lately."

"I'm Martin, that's Mick, Chris and Jackie and this is Dan, he does wines. I would like tonight's menu The team followed Mr Jose into the kitchen where the chefs were busy preparing the nights' menu.

"Mark, Mark!! Chef, are you there?" shouted Mr Jose.

'Mark' thought Martin as he looked at Dan. "I wonder if it's the same Mark who used to work at the "River Gate" a few years ago and got sacked for getting drunk too many times."

"Yes Mr Jose," came the answer from the office at the back of the kitchen.

Dan whispered to Martin, "It's him alright"

"I would like you to come and meet your new head waiter, this is Martin."

The chef came across and shook hands, each pretending not to know each other "Hi chef, this is Dan, Mick, Chris and Jackie. Pleased to meet you."

"I will leave you to get acquainted. I will pop into the restaurant from time to time. If you need anything, I will be in the bar," said Mr Jose, as he headed off to the bar.

"How long have you been here Mark? Is your mate with you?"

"Joe? Yes, he's my second in command. We go everywhere together," said chef.

"What's business like chef?" asked Mick

"Very busy, a lot of chance trade as we are close to the theatre."

"You still like a few glasses of happiness?"

"You better believe it Martin. We all go next door to the "Queens" when we finish. We go in the back way."

Martin gathered all the restaurant staff together and seated them at the big table in the window.

"Good evening, I am your new head waiter, I am only temporary but I require a high standard, I am dividing the restaurant into four. Chris. This is Chris," said Martin, pointing at Chris who was sitting trying to keep a straight face, "you take the two young waiters and look after the tables at the bottom. What are your names?"

"Mario, and he's Luigi"

"That is Chris"

"Mick and Jackie you look after the top end and Dan here will be the wine waiter, any wine or drinks, see him. Mario take Chris, and Jackie and show them where things are, Mick I would like a word."

When they had gone about their duties Martin opened the Restaurant Book and quickly pointed to a party of eight for 7.30pm. Then to another eight at 8.15pm.

"Mick, I am going to make the party at 8.15 vanish. I want you to make sure that you don't let the 7.30 booking leave with their bill. Give the host the change but hold on to the bill. I will give the same bill to the Smith party at table three."

"You had better be careful Martin, you're not Derek Crook."

"Don't worry Mick I will."

The restaurant was pretty full and busy from about 7.00pm. Martin called Dan across.

"Here is a £20 note Dan I want you to keep bringing two pints of lager to the chef and his second every time their glasses get empty."

"But Martin they are half-cut already." Said Dan.

"I know, I know, don't worry I know what I am doing, trust me Dan trust me." smiled Martin.

Everything went well and about 10.15pm table three Mr Smith called Martin across and asked him for the bill.

"Could I have my bill Martin?"

"Certainly Mr Smith, how was your meal tonight?"

"Excellent, Excellent Martin, all my party have enjoyed it, the food was marvellous and of course the service could not be faulted,"

"My chef will be delighted, would you like to thank him yourself?"

"I would indeed" said a slightly intoxicated host.

"Mick could you ask the chef to come out and speak to Mr Smith."

As the chef came into the restaurant and Mick directed him to Mr Smith's table Martin quickly darted into the kitchen to the chef's office and removed the top-copy of table three's order. This meant Martin had both copies, the bottom and top copies of the order. So there was no evidence that there were two parties of eight in the restaurant that night.

"Your bill, Mr Smith," as Martin presented the bill form the previous table of eight to Mr Smith. "There is a 10% service charge on the bill, I would prefer cash if possible, as my machine seems to be on the blink."

"No problem Martin" glancing at the bill for £143 including service. "Here is something for yourself for a drink" slipping Martin a £10 note.

On the way out Mr Lopez was bowing and scraping to the customers as they were leaving.

"Did you enjoy your meal tonight sir," asked Jose.

"Excellent" came the reply from Mr Smith "we will be back."

"I hope so" murmured Martin under his breath. Mr Jose had just treated Mr Smith and his party to an a la carte meal for eight and two bottles of wine.

When the team finished and got paid Mr Jose was delighted and he slipped Martin an extra £5. They nipped in the back door to the bar for last orders.

"How many did we do tonight chef shouted Mick?

"109 covers Mick," answered the chef.

"That's what you think" thought Martin 117 more like it.

When the money got shared out Dan refused his, took a share of the service.

"Give my cut to Billy and Jean"

"Okay Dan, see you tomorrow night"

Next night when the team called into the "Queens" before starting work, Jackie was already there sitting with the two chefs.

"Busy night, tonight Martin" said the chef.

"Good" said Martin taking a sip of his lager.

"Have you three been here all afternoon" said Mick glancing around the table Jackie and the chefs, and the amount of glasses on the table.

"We have had a good session but we will be alright on the night" laughed Joe the second chef.

"I hope so" smiled Dan.

"Martin I don't want anything to do with any more missing bills," said Dan after the chefs had gone to get ready for work.

"I think you're right Dan, but if I got caught we would all be sacked and our reputations would all go down the swanee river. I must admit I'm no Derek Crook."

"Let's just take what's due to us, the tips." said Mick, "I had it all before with that Derek Crook and was very lucky not to get locked up with him."

That night Mr Lopez kept coming in the restaurant picking fault with silly things.

Chris came over to Dan and said "What' the matter with Lopez tonight, if he complains to me anymore about my service I will stick his head in the soup."

"Pay no attention to him. Hurt him where it hurts, in the tip-box, just put a couple of pounds in if you get a fiver or a tenner. Remember the punter wants you to have the money, not him."

About 9.30pm the barman came through to the restaurant.

"Martin, there is a big party of 12 in the bar they say they are booked for 9.15pm and no one has come to take their order," said John.

"There is nothing in the book about a 12, I will come through with the menus in a minute."

"Jackie, can you join those two tables to make a 12, I am going to bring them in straight away."

"Why me Martin? I have been busy all night."

"Don't worry, Chris will help you."

"Who is the main man of the party John" asked Martin.

"Do you need to ask Martin? surely you can hear him over there in the corner at the window, the American guy, I have had a hard time all night, I think they have been drinking before they got here," answered the barman.

"Good evening ladies and gentlemen sorry for the delay, would you like to come through to the restaurant and I will take your order at the table."

"No we would not, we would like you to leave the menus and we will call you when we are ready to order and when the meal is ready we will come through, we will order the wine at the same time." With that he dismissed Martin. Martin was fuming when he returned to the restaurant.

"Cheeky bastard, who does he think he is I will be glad when we are out of here tonight." He said to Dan. He went in the kitchen.

"Chef, we still have a large party to come, I will try and hurry them up but I have a feeling we will have a lot of grief from them." said Martin to the chef who was downing what was probably tenth pint of lager.

"The guy's name is not Grant is it Martin, a big American?"

"Got it in one chef, big head, know him?"

Yeah, sure I do, friend of Lopez, thinks he can do and say what he wants, comes in regular and always says he has booked, he is full of bullshit."

"That's all I need tonight." sighed Martin. "I just hope Jackie stays sober enough to handle this guy Dan, keep an eye on him for me." said Martin.

When the party were seated Martin took the order and then rushed it through to the chef who was totally pissed off as well as being half pissed.

"I hope that chef has everything on the order Dan, most of this party are half drunk. "We could do without the grief" said Martin hopefully.

"Mick you and the two lads finish off the bottom of the restaurant I will sort out the bills Jackie and Chris will look after Mr Grant and Dan will give a hand with the main course, we don't want to be here all night."

"How are you getting on with Mr Grant Jackie" asked Dan.

"Don't ask Dan, he wanted more rolls, more butter, the knife was not sharp enough to cut the rolls. He gave me his soup back telling me it was cold. The woman next to him told him to shut up about three times." sighed Martin.

"Excuse me could you ask that waiter to bloody well hurry up with our main course Martin, we have been waiting about an hour" shouted Mr Grant across at Martin standing at his desk. "I will have to have a word with Mr Lopez about this."

Martin ignored him and a couple of minutes later the swing door from the kitchen swung open and Jackie emerged carrying a huge tray with Chris close behind him with another overloaded tray. Immediately Mr Grant started clapping as did the rest of his party. Jackie just stood there getting redder in the face smiled looked across at Dan looked back to Mr Grant took a step backwards to let go of the tray and began clapping himself. Seeing what Jackie had done Chris dropped his tray and started clapping. Mick looked at Martin, Martin looked at Dan and instinctively they all started clapping, even the two young waiters at the bottom of the restaurant began clapping. Just then the chef and his second staggered through the door to see all their work decorating the carpet. Fillet steaks, Dover Soles, scampi, gravy, tartar sauce, roast potatoes, broccoli, peas, cauliflower and runner beans.

"We're outa here Dan" whispered Martin giving Mick the nod.

"Have you got the wage packets?"

"Yes, I had a funny feeling about tonight so I got the money at 10.30pm."

"We have just time for last orders next door Mick, let's go."

As the team made their quick exit Chris slipped the tip-box under his service cloth.

Mr Grant shouted "What about our meal?"

"There" shouted Jackie pointing to the floor "I hope it's not too cold."

Next door the team stretched out on the comfortable lounge bar chairs.

"Why did you do it Jackie?" asked Mick.

"I don't like Lopez, I don't like Harry, I can't stand people like Grant trying to take the piss, and as for that chef he sent me out with cold soup and I had to wait nearly an hour for the main course, and I was going to miss last orders."

"What about the tips Mick."

"Don't worry, Chris collected them on the way out" laughed Martin.

"So I take it we don't need to be in tomorrow night Mick" asked Chris.

"I think I might give it a miss myself, said Jackie.

"I think you should Jackie" laughed Dan.

"Lopez will be delighted when he comes in tomorrow, I bet he wishes he did not go home early tonight, at least he won't have to spend too much time counting the tips, our tips, we will count our own" smiled Mick.

Next day Harry was on the phone pleading with Dan to go back to the "Park Court" I'm sorry Harry but you didn't tell us about that Lopez paying us with our own money, money the punters gave to us for our excellent service."

"I had no idea Dan, he told me he would pay the team £5 an hour."

"Bollocks Harry, you knew the score, Lopez had been ripping waiting staff off for years, all you were interested in was your fee, you and Jack can go tonight, see how you like having to steal your own tips. Don't bother ringing the others we just took what was ours and split, must go, see you later."

CHAPTER 12

A SPIRITUAL EXPERIENCE

Dan phoned Mick.

"Harry's been on the phone begging again Mick, I told him to go to "The Park" himself. He wasn't too pleased, anyway fancy coming around this evening to watch the match? Bring Chris, Joan and James have gone to Butlins."

"I'll give Martin a ring, can we bring some beer?"

"I don't mind as long as you don't expect me to have any, bring me a big bottle of Coke, and see you about seven."

The talk was about Harry and Lopez.

"Hope Harry is not too busy tonight" said Chris laughing.

"Serves him right! Wouldn't it be funny if Lopez caught him stealing his own tips?" said Dan.

"Do you not drink at all now Dan?" asked Chris as he opened another can.

"Not since I stopped being a monk" laughed Dan.

"A Monk Dan? Were you a monk? asked Chris.

"Oh, he was a Monk alright Chris, he was nicknamed Rasputin," laughed Martin "you have heard of Rasputin the mad monk haven't you, a womanising, pissed up monk in Russia? Well Dan was the equivalent in Yorkshire."

"You're having me on Martin" said Chris.

"I don't know what you and Mick are laughing at Martin you were monks as well" said Dan laughing.

"Yeah, but you were the Abbott" said Martin. "Go on Dan tell Chris about the monks cellar."

"Okay, I'll go make a jug of coffee and Chris I want you to keep this story to yourself.

I have taken a lot of stick over the years, and don't dare call me

Rasputin" laughed

Dan as he went into the kitchen.

"A lot of years ago when I was still drinking, a new hotel not far away were looking for a bar manager so I applied. I went for the interview and got the job, which was running a late night cellar bar. The hotel manager mentioned he would need another barman, so I phoned Martin and he got the job."

"We both still had no idea what we had got ourselves into, did we Dan? Mr Tate the manger only said it was to be a theme bar under the hotel, opening at 6.30pm and closing at 1.00am and we could have a bedroom if we felt like not travelling home."

"Yore right Martin, I could not believe the money! I think if was £8 an hour, of course we were not to find out why we were paid so well."

"What happened Dan" asked Chris.

"Both Martin and I arrived the day before and we were sitting in the foyer waiting for Mr Tate and these two cleaners walked by looked at us and started to laugh,"

"I remember saying to Dan 'is there something you're not telling me' you just laughed"

"I honestly had no idea what was coming next Martin."

"This head waiter was passing and he stopped and said "are you two the monks then"

I looked at you and you looked at me and before we could say anything Mr Tate came out of his office.

"Good morning gents, shall we go downstairs." With that he headed downstairs and we followed. "This is it, what do you think?" Martin looked at me; and pointed to the sign above the bar.

'Welcome to "The Monks Cellar"

"I remember what you said to Tate Dan"

"I don't believe this, next thing you will be asking us to wear habits."

"Got it in one Dan, after I show you around you can collect your habits, I mean uniforms from the linen room, I have your badges in my office." said Tate with a wry smile on his face.

"Remember the other sign Dan, "To the Convent?" You should do! You spent a lot of time there. We spent all morning stocking up the bar, polishing the tables we must have drank about a bottle of brandy before two o'clock."

"When we collected our habits you had a white one as well."

"That was because at 1.00am I changed from the brown habit into the Abbott's white habit which meant the bar was closed."

"What was the convent like Martin?" asked Chris.

"It was just a storeroom a long a corridor, Dan could tell you better about the convent" laughed Martin.

"You have got to understand Chris there was a large space for dancing surrounded with tables and chairs with the disco in the comer. The music came from the roof. It was really for rich kids from the surrounding areas, the drinks were expensive to keep out the riffraff. It was a hit from night one, so much so that we phoned Mick, he became monk number three, Mick will take up the story I am going to put the kettle on." said Dan laughing.

"When I arrived the following Saturday night I walked down the steps into the cellar and I was greeted by these two monks, Brother Dan behind the bar, and Brother Martin this side of the bar. Dan described the set up. He worked behind the bar, Martin and I would be in charge of the tables, all drinks were served by us. I got changed in the convent and was presented with a badge, Brother Mick. When Dan wanted a break one of us relieved him, which turned out to be a lot"

"Did you get many tips Mick?"

"Many tips Chris? What do you think? We made a load! we handed them over the bar to Dan who put them in a glass and kept the drinks flowing, we always had Special Brew at the corner of the bar. You just pulled your hood over so no-one could see you drinking, so you can imagine how popular it was to see three pissed up monks running a bar."

"Tell Chris about Nicole, Dan" smiled Martin.

"Ah, Nicole, every night about 9.30pm, after the boss came down to see how business was going and then headed home I used to come out and get the DJ to play all my type of music and I would be boogieing with all the girls. That's when Nicole came along. She was beautiful she was a regular, with a gang of her pals who came every Friday and Saturday night. One Saturday night she came up to me at the bar and said "will you give me a dance tonight Brother Dan, I'm Nicole, I'm sitting over there" pointing to a group of girls in the corner.

I had a couple of large brandies and got Martin to stand in while I went out to boogie.

I always got the DJ to play Gloria by Van Morrison. Anyway, Nicole asked what went on in the convent so I said "Come with me Nicole and I will show you," I did not have to ask a second time" I brought her into the store room come convent and behind the door I slipped my skirt up and also hers, she came well prepared suspenders and stockings, There I was with my skirt up and my hood back having a knee trembler with this classy girl in the convent, I will always remember her whispering in my ear in her posh accent. "Oh you are naughty Brother Dan, wait till I tell all my friends I have been fucked by a monk" and she did. That's how I got the name Rasputin."

"You won't believe what he did next, he only got the manager to put a bed in the store room saying because of the noise in the cellar he was getting migraine headaches and needed to lay down for about 10 minutes till the headache cleared, what a wally he was to believe that story. You can guess what he used the bed for, ha ha."

"Surely with the amount you three were drinking the stocks were down" quizzed Chris.

"The stocks would not have been good if Martin did not come up with a classic. He had been talking to the Banqueting Bar Manager, whom after a good few drinks let slip that he had quite a few big banquets and all drinks were to be charged to the accounts and nobody was to pay cash. So he had been adding £200 to each drinks bill, so his stock would be sky high. On hearing this we decided to relieve him of some stock that had already been paid for.

"The floor above is the ground floor and that is where the beer and wine cellar was. We would put a requisition to the cellar-man and he would put the stock in the hoist and send it down to us. He did the same to the banqueting bar at the second floor, well Chris, what goes up comes down and what comes down like the hoist goes up again." smiled Mick.

"So what did you do Mick" asked Chris opening another beer.

"Martin had this wonderful idea of relieving Larry, the Banqueting Manager, of some of his ill-gotten paid for booze. One night after we had closed and Dan was cashing up he went behind the bar and pressed the button on the hoist and brought it down. He took the shelf out and called Dan."

"Fancy a trip up to the Banqueting suite Brother Dan? I think we could be doing with a stock injection. The stock check is Saturday and if we don't we will all be looking for another Monastery.

"Why me Martin?" Asked Dan.

"You're the smallest and I get a bit claustrophobic, all you have got to do is climb in, I will press the button and send you up past the stock room to the Banqueting Bar, fill the hoist send it down. We will empty it and send it back up for you, when you are back in safely, knock and I will bring you back down." said Martin.

"I remember thinking what a good idea and climbed in and Martin sent me up. It seemed like an age but when I got to the top, I gently opened the two doors and peeped out. There had not been any function on that night and the only light was behind the bar. I climbed out and quickly found the stash of knocked off bottles the banqueting manager had been bragging about I put about twenty bottles of brandy and whiskey into the hoist together with two cases of Carlsberg larger and sent it down to Martin. He unloaded the hoist sent it back up and I got in and closed the door, banged the side, and down I came." smiled Dan.

"And that solved the stock problem Chris, but things just went from bad to worse, we were all drinking far too much. Martin was getting pissed up and pissed off with Brother Dan doing less work, just dancing and screwing. Anyway on Saturday when we came in early to stock up and tidy the bar, Brother Dan announced he was leaving next Saturday to check into a rehab clinic to dry out and stop drinking." said Mick.

"Chris, I was in a bad state, seldom eating and just drinking, I went to see the manager next day told him, due to my migraines my doctor advised me to pack in work. He did not seem to be bothered and told me he had decided to close the Monks Cellar because of complaints about the music and the noise by the hotel guests who could not get to sleep. We had a farewell party the next Saturday and I was dressed in my white habit of the Abbot. I kept both habits when we left. I went into the clinic shortly after and when I came out I went to AA and I have never drank since Chris."

"Does it not bother you with us drinking here in your house Dan?" asked Chris.

"No Chris, not in the least" said Dan.

"I wish I could do what you did Dan, I have been going downhill steadily for years I must stop." said Mick opening another Special Brew.

"When you have had enough I will help you Mick, if AA worked for me it will work for you, but you have to want to stop more than anything and maybe you haven't wanted it enough." said Dan. "Anyway can we watch what's left of the match now" laughed Martin "that is if that's all right with the Abbott."

Harry's agency acquired nearly all of Maria's Black and White agency staff and she was none too pleased Although she made out she was glad to be rid of "The River Gate", she was furious at losing the business. She phoned Mick.

"Who's this new agency Mick, who is behind it?"

"I don't know Maria, all I know is the new G.M. has decided he was unhappy with the reports about some of your staff knocking and especially on the banqueting side. His exact words were, on watching a function, "those agency staff are crap." That was the night before he officially took over."

'They will be back. You will still work for us Mick won't you?"

"You know me Maria, I go where there is work, cash in hand, keep in touch."

Mick did not want to say too much to Maria especially as she had sent Harry to work with Mick on the Christmas parties a couple of years ago, but he also knew that word would get back to her eventually but he did not want to be the bearer of bad tidings.

Darren on the banqueting department was over the moon with his new staff, having got rid of most of his older staff upstairs to "The Anchor Restaurant" with Pablo and Pedro. Mr Tropez was top class, the team held him in the highest respect. He was the best manager the team had known. He liked Harry and he could see that Harry was not all that he was made out to be. He knew Harry had not worked in catering long although Harry tried to make out he had been as long as Dan in the business. Mr Tropez dressed immaculately, he had style, he knew everything about the hotel industry, always listened to his staff's point of view. He once told Dan 'If you have a problem come straight to me I'm the manager.' Dan liked that. He got rid of some staff he thought were, as he put it, 'have not got "The River Gate" at heart'.

"Hello Dan, is Joan there."

"Joan, Harry is on the phone."

"Hi Harry, what's up, you don't usually phone me."

"Joan, I'm in deep shit, I took a booking a couple of months ago for a cricket club annual dinner near Bradford, I have nearly all my staff booked out, I was wondering if you could run the function for me. It's for 120 people and I have got some staff, waitresses, you may know some, and I have Jackie."

"There is just one thing Harry I don't have a car yet".

"Don't worry, I'll lend you mine, get a taxi over to my house. I'll phone Jackie and you can pick him up outside the "Alhambra Theatre.""

"I hope I am getting extra money for all this messing about, why don't you ask Dan."

"You know me Joan, I'll see you right, I have Dan in "The Gate" tonight. I need him there as I won't be, as I am taking my good lady out for her birthday."

"It's nearly 4.00pm now Harry you don't give me much time, see you at your house at 6pm. Bye."

Joan picked up Harry's car and headed for Bradford to pick up Jackie at "The Alhambra".

Jackie was there, Joan parked up and he got in.

"I thought you were Harry, Joan."

"Do I look like Harry, Jackie?"

"How could you miss it Jackie, it's falling apart, you hear it before you see it."

"Don't you get pissed up on me tonight Jackie."

"Don't worry I won't"

When they arrived Harry's staff were already there laying tables up. Joan recognised some. "Hi everybody, Harry has put me in charge tonight but since you all know the job there should be no problems. I hope."

"Good evening, I'm Mr Austin the club secretary we have about 120 and they do get a bit impatient, but pay no attention, the wives are worse."

"What time do you sit down?" "8pm sharp, we have a lot to get through what with presentations."

"All right everyone gather round, where's Jackie?"

"Jackie, over here, I want you on food, you put the plates down, Ruth on roast beef,

Ann and Mary veg., you two young girls do gravy and horseradish sauce."

"Why can't I do wines Joan?"

"Their bar staff are doing all the drinks and you have had enough anyway Jackie."

"Right now everybody. Let's get in the melon starters, put them straight down on the tables."

"I will do the top table, so keep your eye on me, when you see me lift the plates you lift, straight in the kitchen for the plates Jackie, and Ruth and Anne and Mary you follow."

"Excuse me Joan I am sorry to tell you we will be running about 40 minutes late our President has just left home now."

"Is there any where we can sit down and have a cup of tea Mr Austin?"

"Yes there is a little tea room through the bar."

When the meal got underway everything looked like Jean was going to have a nice trouble free night. Jackie headed out with his plates, the girls followed with the food. With just one table to do, Joan was thinking about what an easy job this was when there was an almighty roar from a lady at the table, she looked down just in time to see Jackie vanish out the side door, taking his dickie-bow off. She rushed down to see what was wrong. Ruth and Anne moved back to reveal two slices of beef, carrots and peas, placed neatly on the table-cloth.

"What happened here" said an astonished Joan.

The waiter who just went through that door was a plate short so he just took out his pen and leaned over and drew a plate on the cloth and those two silly women put the meal on the cloth, and that young girl was just about to pour gravy on it, do something, do something." screamed the irate woman.

"Get a plate Ruth and clear this mess and Anne put a small table cloth in front of this lady. See the chef and get another meal, I am going to strangle that Jackie."

There was no sign of Jackie when the meal finished and Mr Austin came across to Joan.

"Wait till I see that Harry Green, he told me he would send me top class staff. You are the only one who knew what was happening. He sends me a couple of grannies and their families and a half drunk waiter.

As Joan was about to drive off she noticed Jackie slumped in the doorway next to the pub by the cricket club. She pulled up opened the window and shouted. "You bastard, you have caused me a load of grief, you can bloody well walk home."

With that she drove off. About a mile up the road she stopped the car and started laughing. "Drew a bloody plate on the cloth and those two dummies put the meal on it"

With that she turned the car and went back to where Jackie was slumped in the doorway. "Are you coming or what Jackie." Jackie climbed in, sulking he dozed off.

CHAPTER 13

EXIT HARRY AND THE 2 P'S

When Joan got home she had a talk with Dan about the fiasco at the cricket club with Jackie and the staff Harry had sent.

"Dan, I think we should give some thought about working for Harry. We don't need him, we have always done well on our own."

"But Joan, the majority of our work is at "The River Gate" and Harry sends the staff and so far Pablo is happy with him, as is Darren in banqueting."

"You are well thought of by Mr. Tropez. Why don't you see if you can do something?"

"I think I will give Darren a ring tomorrow."

Next day Dan phoned Darren.

"Darren, Harry's got to go, I am going to speak to the rest of the team, I want you to speak to Mr. Tropez and see if you can pay us cash and blow Harry out."

"But it was you who got him into "The Gate" Dan, what am I going to say?"

"Tell Mr. Tropez Harry is costing too much for his staff and that we will work for you without Harry, and how much money you could save by paying us £1 per hour more, cutting him out although he could work as a waiter if he wanted."

"Leave it with me Dan, I'll be in touch."

Dan phoned Martin and asked him what he thought about blowing Harry's agency out.

"Why not Dan, I've seen some of the old grannies he sent to that Masonic dinner last week. I saw Mr. Tropez taking notes, some of them could hardly walk."

"Tell Martin about Jackie's performance Dan."

"Leave it Joan, we will sort it."

Next day Darren called the team up to his office after breakfast. Jackie was also there trying to hide in the comer. When they were all comfortable Darren left his office and returned with Mr. Tropez.

"Darren has spoken to me about your decision to discontinue working for the agency and work on a casual basis for the hotel. I am a businessman and from a business point of view I am pleased, also why should anyone get any of your hard-earned money? You are the best staff and Darren is pleased.

You can discuss the money with him. I will speak to Harry. As from first of next month he is out."

"Thank you very much Mr. Tropez, we must get back and get ready for lunch."

"Thanks Darren, see you later, we are not in for you until Friday night. Bye."

"See you Dan."

"Say nothing to Harry about our talk Martin. I will next Friday night"

"OK Darren."

During lunch Jackie kept a very low profile.

"Martin, have you noticed how quiet Jackie is after his classic the other night."

"But Dan, Jackie is always quiet, I'm going to ask him about it."

"Hi Jackie, what happened at the cricket club?"

"It was a rubbish job, I didn't want to go anyway, that Harry talked me into it, like he does. He sent a couple of his old grannies and their granddaughters, then the secretary announced he would be late, so that meant I would have missed last orders next door, then when we finally got going I only forgot a plate. I thought, I have had enough, but they added another punter to the last table and didn't tell me. So it was too late to go the whole way back, so I just took my pen out and drew one, and left them to it. I now understand the two silly old moos behind me put the meal on the cloth. I wish I'd have seen that, but the bar next door was more important at the time. I did feel sorry for Joan but eventually she saw the funny side. I have always wanted to do that. I didn't like the secretary, I didn't want to be there and I don't like Harry anyway."

The talk in "Maggie's" after lunch was all about Jackie but Mick had some very exciting news for the team.

"Do you remember Pablo telling us about having the builders in at his new house?"

"I remember Mick, that was months ago, why?"

"Well Dan, they only converted the whole basement into a bistro and they opened it last week. They take turns about running it. Pablo does the rotas so that Pedro works lunches and he does dinners at "The River Gate.""

"They kept that quiet Martin."

"I told you Dan that Pablo was clever, he will have his own agenda, but it does surprise me he never told us." "But I haven't told you the best bit." "Go on Mick, tell us." "Harry has only been sending staff there." "I don't believe it, who?"

"Just a couple of young girls, they have been at "The Gate" a couple of times, I don't know their names."

"Harry is going to need Pablo's bistro after next month, but it just shows you how deceitful he is."

"Do you know where it is Mick?"

"Yes, he told me his house was just past the traffic lights on our way home."

"Fancy calling in for a drink on the way home?"

"Why not, we might find Harry doing lunch."

"Let's go Martin, see you lot later."

"See you Dan."

About a mile down the road home they come to the traffic lights.

"It's around here somewhere Dan." "I don't believe it Martin, look." "Where?" "Down there, look at the sign. "The 2 P's." "Are we going in?"

"Why not, park here."

Martin and Dan went down the steps and into the bistro and over to the small bar to be greeted by a very camp barman.

"Can I be of service gents?"

"I don't think so," smiled Dan. "We would like to have a word with your boss."

"Pedro dear, somebody to see you."

Just then Pedro appeared wearing a multi-coloured shirt.

"Hello my friends, nice to see you, Stephan give my friends a drink."

"Half a lager and a coke for Dan, thank you Pedro."

"You kept this quiet Pedro."

"We did, didn't we, but it is really for gays Dan, so we didn't think there was any point. Come, I will show you around. We have 12 tables, can seat 60 punters, a little dance floor and disco, a well-stocked bar and come through and meet the chef. Hi chef, these are my friends from "The Gate", Martin and Dan and keep off - they're straight!"

"Dan if you need any work give me a ring."

"Some chance Pedro."

"Now we don't have to be like that Dan."

"Dan, have you seen anything familiar, look around."

"Holy shit Martin, I have just noticed, the lamps on the tables, the pictures, the cloths on the tables and even the napkins, they're the same as "The River Gate!"

"You naughty boy Pedro, I suppose when the cloths get stained you use "The River Gate" laundry."

"Exactly, we just bring the stained table-cloths and napkins to "The Gate" and exchange them. Listen, I must do the bill for that table in the comer, have your drinks, I will see you at "The Gate" on Friday."

"Let's go Martin, we don't want to be seen here."

"You're right Dan, see you later Pedro."

About three weeks later, Mr. Tropez's secretary and her boyfriend went for lunch at a new bistro called "The 2P's", not knowing who owned it. What a shock to see Pablo and two of Harry's staff from "The Gate". Of course after lunch, having eaten on the same table-cloths, same plates, drank from the same glasses as "The Gate", even admired the same pictures that hung in her own office, Pablo phoned Pedro to tell him the shit would hit the fan when Mr. Tropez found out, which he did. He knew he could be done for theft, so a decision was made that afternoon to close and the shutters went up.

Harry phoned Dan, not knowing Dan knew he was for the sack.

"Dan, I'm in deep shit. That Pablo has closed his bistro and pissed off without paying me my money."

"What money Harry?" said Dan.

"I have been sending some staff to his new bistro and now he has shut up shop, I am left out of pocket."

"Harry, you kept that quiet, I understand neither Pablo nor Pedro turned up at "The Gate" last night, so it looks like we will be looking for another restaurant manager."

"What should I do then Dan?"

"Listen Harry, I will be truthful with you, we all know you were sending staff to Pablo's, your problem is convincing Mr. Tropez that you have very bad eyesight."

"Why is that Dan?"

"Don't act stupid Harry, You have been in Pablo's. Everything he had in there came from "The River Gate", even the staff he had come from you. Are you going to explain to Mr. Tropez you never noticed anything familiar there?"

"I'll say I got the booking for staff by phone and I had not been there."

"You do that Harry, you do that, anyway I am going to have my tea now, good luck Harry, bye."

"Do you think he will believe me Dan?"

"What do you think, bye."

"Good morning Mr. Tropez."

"Good morning Harry, glad you could come in to see me at such short notice.

I have asked you to come in as there is a small matter I would like you to clear up for me."

"I will do my best Mr. Tropez," said Harry sheepishly.

"You have been sending staff that generally come here to a bistro called "The 2P's", owned and jointly run by my Restaurant Manager and Head Waiter."

"As you will now be aware both Pablo and Pedro have vanished, probably camping it up on the Algarve and have left me with some major staff problems."

"That's where I can help you perhaps, Mr. Tropez."

"No Harry, no. I suppose you will tell me you have not been to the bistro, so you would not have seen all the stolen property from this hotel."

"Honestly Mr. Tropez, Pablo phoned me and I sent him some staff."

"Harry don't insult my intelligence, all I ask of people who work for me is loyalty. I have not had that from you, so I have made a decision. As from the first of the month I will not be using your agency again, so you can arrange to send your invoice to the wages clerk and you will be paid what you are owed."

"But Mr. Tropez"...

"But Mr. Tropez nothing, Harry. Goodbye."

The talk in "Maggie's" after breakfast was all about Harry's exit and the vanishing "2P's".

"We passed by this morning and the shutters were up, weren't they Martin?"

"Yes Dan, but we were sure we saw Harry chasing two gay guys up the street shouting "where's my money," said Martin laughing.

"Here comes Darren, Mick, this will be good."

"Good morning everyone, I can't stay long but I just came around to tell you I have sorted out with the accountant how you will get paid, I told her you all would be paying your own tax, was that right?"

"But of course Darren."

"All the waitresses downstairs will be coming upstairs and you lot will be working primarily for me, but maybe sometimes in "The Anchor" restaurant.

Must go, see you Friday."

CHAPTER 14

BROWN ENVELOPE

Sitting in "Maggie's" after lunch the next day, all the talk was about Jan and Jill's' performance in Manchester.

"I have never been so embarrassed in my life," said Jean," but to make matters worse, the punters started shouting at me to get up on the table too, didn't they Billy?"

"Why didn't you, Jean? The two girls made a fortune," answered Billy laughing.

"Piss off Billy, I still have some standards to live up to. Knocking about with you is as low as I'm going."

"Hi Jack! You and that Harry got any jobs for male strippers?" laughed Billy.

"Don't blame us, we had nothing to do with that job. Anyway, I have some nice little breakfast jobs coming up, no stoppers need apply," replied Jack.

Jack was a family man with two children at college. His wife, Anne, had had polio as a child, and he liked to stay as close to her as possible, he would not work away.

Martin and Jack were in the same boat. They would like to work full time but had to settle for benefits with some cash in hand but now Jack was the front man for Harry's agency he'd had to give up the giro and this caused rows at home with Anne so he had to do more jobs himself.

"Hi Harry! How does it feel to be a waiter again at "The Gate" after all those fees you charged for us and yourself?" shouted Chris, mockingly.

"Leave us alone Chris, can't you see I'm in deep discussions with my partner Jack about trying to get you all some work," said Harry with his poor face on.

"Where are these breakfasts then Jack," said Mick," and when are we getting paid?"

"They're for Georgio, at "The Hydro," said Harry.

"I'll do some Jack, and so will Chris. What about you Billy?" said Mick.

"You seem keen Mick, do you know the guy?" asked Billy.

"Sure, he's a cool dude, one of us, he'll see us right. Hey Jack, is Georgio paying us?"

"Yes, after each meal," answered Jack.

"How many does he need Harry?"

"Only three the first week and four the second," said Harry, "probably for a few weeks."

"Us three will go the first week. It will be good to see Georgio again," said Mick.

"Anyway, I'm off to see my kids, anybody want a lift?" asked Mick.

"Hold on, I'm coming," shouted Chris, "I have to go to the post office and it's not to cash a Giro."

"See you Chris," laughed Billy.

"The Hydro" was a big hotel on the outskirts of the city that specialised in conferences and weddings. Georgio had been the manager for a few years now but he could not keep staff long, especially waitresses. He was a smallish man, about 44, quite attractive and a smart dresser, from Sicily. His second wife Anna was a waitress who had run off with the barman. His first wife was Italian and she went home to Italy because she could not stand any more affairs. Mick had worked for him casually a few times. Georgio was having a lot of trouble finding breakfast staff. He only had three staff to do 150 guests so that is why he'd called Jack.

 "On our way back home tonight why don't we call in and find out the score from Georgio," asked Chris.

"Okay but only one drink Chris, you know how knackered I always am after I've taken the boys out," answered Mick.

That night Mick, Chris, Billy and Jean called into "The Hydro" after they'd finished at "The Gate". The staff bar was busy as usual, Georgio was at his usual corner, holding up the bar, talking to a pretty girl.

"Hey Georgio, what's going down?" shouted Mick.

"Mick, my old friend, good to see you! Who're your friends? Hi, Angel, give Mick and his friends a drink on my account. Long time no see, are you coming to work for me?"

"We're going to do some breakfasts for you next week. This is Chris, Billy and Jean. What's the matter, you been interfering with your waitresses again?" laughed Mick.

"How's Dan and Martin doing?" asked Georgio," heard they'd become monks!"

"Everybody must have heard about that, Georgio. They have given up wearing frocks now, you'll probably see them in a couple of weeks," laughed Mick. "Anyway, we're not staying long. I have a long day with my kids again tomorrow."

"You still seeing that woman, Mick? I thought you'd have left her long ago, she was a bit crazy," said Georgio.

"A bit crazy!" mumbled Chris.

"I don't live with her now, I just go to see the kids," said Mick.

"Not getting married again are you Georgio?" asked Mick, looking at the attractive blonde next to him.

"No way," smiled Georgio.

After a couple of drinks they said their farewells and headed home.

"Seems a nice guy that Georgio," said Chris to Mick.

"He is Chris, just another casualty of the catering industry," said Mick.

The restaurant was large with a carvery in the middle and a cold buffet at the side. It overlooked some beautiful gardens.

"Good morning, you must be from the agency, my name is Sandra, and I'm the breakfast supervisor."

"Hi! I'm Mick, this is Chris and that's Billy. We are here for three mornings and I would appreciate it if you could have our money ready at eleven when we finish, we have another job to go to and don't want to be kept hanging around,"

"I don't know anything about paying you, the agency will be doing that," said Sandra turning her nose up.

"You'd better find out dear or you'll be doing these breakfasts yourself," said Chris.

Sandra could see that they meant it, she was not talking to some students now. She nodded, mumbled something and headed off to the reception to see the duty manager about the cash.

"You would not have to be a genius to work out why there is a shortage of staff here," said Billy to Mick.

Sandra was about 24, a bit overweight, with no style and a bad attitude.

"She is definitely in the wrong business Chris, you can see that she does not like people. Anyway, as long as she stays out of the way I'm not bothered," said Mick.

"I wonder how she has reigned for so long?" asked Chris.

"Maybe Georgio is giving her one, Chris," added Mick.

As breakfast started to get busy the two full time staff began dumping the dirty bowls and plates on the drops Chris was working from.

"Hi you two, don't leave your dirty plates on my drop, take them into the kitchen."

Chris wasn't too keen on working with students anyway. They duly obliged even though they were not students.

"Have you noticed that bird just sits behind that desk and when some guests arrive at the door she puts her head down and one of us has got to greet and seat them. Surely that's what she's paid to do, Mick?" quizzed Chris.

"Don't let her get to you Chris, we're only here for three days," laughed Mick.

"What's your names?" Billy asked the two full time staff.

"I'm Kate and that's Lisa," said Kate.

"How many more staff have you got Kate?" asked Billy

c

"We have five more on breakfast, three are part time and two are full time, like us," answered Kate.

"Where are they today?" "One is on holiday, two on days off and two off sick, I'll be surprised if they come back anyway."

"What's wrong here Kate?" asked Mick who was standing close by.

"Her for a start," snapped Lisa under her breath pointing at Sandra seated behind her desk.

"And the tips," said Kate. "We do about four hours a week for breakfast and the courier comes in and hands her a brown envelope with money in it which is supposed to be shared amongst us but we never see any and around every three months we get about a tenner."

"It's no wonder you are short staffed Kate. I will have a chat with Chris and see what we can do," smiled Mick.

After breakfast Billy headed home to Jean, and Mick and Chris went for a game of pool at "Maggie's". The place was very quiet and Mick asked Paul the barman if Dan had been in. "Yes, Dan's not long gone but he said he'd be back at 12.00 to meet Joan. I think they are doing a little lunch at "The Gate."

"He's probably gone to put his bet on," said Chris.

"He'll end up going to Gamblers Anonymous as well as AA." laughed Mick.

"Dan's not that bad yet but he does win Mick. I worked with him last year when he won two grand and he had a thousand in each pocket He could not leave it at home in case Joan found it and he could not put it in the bank because he owed the bank a load of money," said Chris. "You know that Skoda Joan drives, Dan bought it out of that money but Joan thinks he got a loan from the bank. Here comes Joan now, say nothing, tell her Dan's just gone to the shop for a paper."

"Hi Chris, hi Mick! I thought you two were doing breakfasts at "The Hydro?" said Joan as she walked over to the two guys sitting in the corner.

"We finished at 11.00am and came over for a game of pool before going home, you and Dan doing lunch at "The Gate?" asked Chris.

"Yes we are when he arrives. I hope he's not in that bookies again."

"He's just gone over for a paper Joan," said Chris.

"That'll be right. Anyway, I'll give him five minutes and then I'm off."

"How's the car going, Joan?" asked Paul the barman.

"I get a lot of stick because it's a Skoda but it gets us to jobs and we don't have to rely on other people especially Martin for lifts."

"Why Martin," asked Paul

"Every time there is a full moon he goes on a bender and you don't see him for days.

Dan and I have stood many times waiting to get picked up and he hasn't showed. We lost a lot of credibility due to him, but it was our own fault, we should have known better," said Joan.

"You have no room to talk Joan. How many times have you taken jobs and gone on the piss and I have had to make excuses?" said Dan as he joined them.

"Oh you're here then," said Joan sarcastically, "well did you win then?"

"Win what Joan?"

"Don't try and kid me Dan. I know you'll have been over to put a bet on the morning dogs at Hackney," smiled Joan.

"What's the score at "The Hydro" Mick? We are there next week," asked Dan.

"It's a nice hotel, about 140 rooms and it caters mostly for conferences in the winter and weddings and tours in the summer. It seems they are now doing two tours a night, every two nights, so it looks like there may be plenty of work there, as long as they keep the breakfast supervisor."

"What do you mean," asked Joan

"She's called Sandra and she gives the breakfast staff a hard time with her attitude so they don't stay long. I think that's why we are there now, but wait until you here the best part, she is only pocketing the couriers tip," laughed Chris.

"What do the other staff say about it?" asked Joan

"It seems she tells the part time staff that they are not entitled to any tips and the three full time girls that there is only a fiver in the brown envelope and that goes in the tip box and is shared every three months."

"But we know the standard tip the courier gives in his envelope is 50p per tourist so if there is the average tour of 50 people staying for two nights it's £25 and there are three tours a week. That is £75 in the envelope. So she puts £15 per week in the box and pockets sixty pounds." said Dan.

"She must be in it with the head waiter, have you met him yet Mick?" asked Joan

"No, it was his day off but he's in tomorrow. His name is Nasser and he's Egyptian.

He starts at 10.30am, just before we go at 11.00am. From what the two girls, Kate and Lisa, say, when he comes in they both head for a cig and a coffee laughing and joking together," said Chris.

"Probably going up to split the tips," smiled Mick. "Those two girls work very hard. I think we might have to teach that Sandra a lesson like we did that German head waiter a few years ago."

"Dan, you and Martin are there next week, it should be no problem. She's not yet met you so she'll be none the wiser."

Dan remembered the German head waiter a few years back at "The Gate" who used to get a brown envelope each day the tour would leave from the courier. He'd put it in his pocket and say nothing to anyone until one day Dan got a pleasant surprise when a new courier gave him the tip instead of the head waiter. Dan had a quiet word with him to be very discreet and give him the envelope each time he brought the tour. The courier had a word with the other couriers so Dan received them all, which he shared with all the staff to the amazement of the head waiter, his fiddle was uncovered so he left.

"I'll ring Martin tonight and tell him the score. Joan and I are off now, we have a nice little buffet lunch at "The Gate", see you later."

"Come on you, we'll be late. Once you start talking you never stop," Joan said to Dan.

"There are a lot of people in the local cemetery who would like to talk like me Joan," answered Dan as they headed off.

Mick, Chris and Billy did the rest of the breakfasts that week. Nothing changed, the couriers gave the brown envelope to Sandra as usual and there were no complaints.

Mick was going to mention it to Georgio but thought he'd be better leaving it to Dan and Martin to sort her out. All he could hear from Chris was 'thieving bitch'.

On Monday when Dan, Chris and Martin arrived there were two tours for breakfast and Chris had explained the situation to Dan and Martin. Sandra was just like Chris had described, she came across to Dan and began explaining how to serve breakfasts.

"You two work with the tours at that end of the restaurant and Chris, you were here last week, and you work with the two girls Kate and Lisa at the top looking after the big paying guests."

Martin looked at Dan, smiled and headed down to the bottom of the restaurant.

"We've got a right one here Dan, don't say anything, I can see you are a bit agitated"

"I don't like her attitude Martin, we'll have to bring her down a peg or two."

"We will Dan, we will," said Martin, "you just keep an eye out for the courier and watch what happens."

Martin and Dan decided to keep a low profile and get on with serving the Australian tourists with their breakfasts. When the courier came in he recognised Martin immediately.

"Martin my friend, how are you? What are you doing here?"

"Juan, it's good to see you again. It's quiet at "The River Gate" so I'm doing my friend a favour. How often do you stop here?" asked Martin

"Twice a week. We go up to Edinburgh tomorrow and back again at the end of the week," said Juan.

"You still give the old brown envelope?" asked Martin

"Oh yes, it is part of the deal with the hotels, one pound per tourist when we go. You should know Martin, I've given you a few brown envelopes over the years," laughed Juan.

"How does your wife like you being away from Madrid all these years, she may have someone else, Juan?" laughed Martin.

"No chance Martin, she loves me."

"Excuse me, would you mind getting on with your work; we don't pay you to stand talking," interrupted Sandra in her ignorant voice.

"Sorry about that," answered Martin, winking at Juan, and he began collecting the dirty breakfast plates.

"When do we get our breakfast?" asked Dan.

"When the tours have gone and you've laid up the tables for lunch - about 10 o'clock if you get on with it and stop talking so much," said Sandra.

Dan smiled and thought *you won't be so smart when we take you down a peg or two.'

When Dan and Martin went for breakfast in the staff room, Chris joined them.

"You were right about that supervisor Sandra, Chris," said Dan.

'Tomorrow I will get Juan to give me the brown envelope and I will switch it for one with a tenner and then pass it on to Sandra. There should be about £40 in the original one so she will be well pleased when she goes to open it and shares it with her head waiter," said Martin.

"Surely she'll be waiting and watching for the courier in the morning," said Chris.

"Don't worry Chris, Dan will distract her," said Martin.

When the waiters returned to the restaurant Sandra went for her breakfast and Martin went into the foyer and spoke to Juan.

"I would like you to do me a favour Juan. I would like you to give me the brown envelope tomorrow morning, to give to Sandra. I will give it to her. It does not matter but it would be better if she saw you doing it," said Martin.

"What are you up to Martin?"

"I am just making sure Lisa and Kate get their tips," winked Martin.

Next morning Dan and Martin agreed Chris would work with Martin, and Dan would work with Lisa and Kate, so he could keep his eye on Sandra.

"Hi Sandra, I'll work with the two girls today. Chris works better with Martin and tours," said Dan.

"Suit yourself, as long as the job gets done."

And with that she walked over to her desk and pretended to do some paper work.

The Australian tourists arrived in the restaurant at 7.30am prompt, as they always do on these coach tours, starving. Juan sat on his own at the side. Martin and Chris put large flasks of coffee and tea and baskets of toast on the tables. The tourists demolished the buffet, as usual.

Chris told Dan to make sure Sandra saw Juan handing Martin the brown envelope. When Juan was about to leave the restaurant he walked towards Martin with the envelope held out in front.

"Excuse me Sandra, Do you want me to give them a hand to lay up down there?" said Dan.

Sandra looked up just in time to see the brown envelope land in Martin's hand. Martin walked straight up to her.

"The courier's just given me this envelope Sandra, I think it's for you."

Sandra grabbed it with a sigh of relief.

"Thanks Martin, you can get back to work." She stuck the envelope in her pocket.

Walking back down the restaurant smiling, he winked at Chris, opening his hand to show him the original brown envelope. When the head waiter came in they both headed up to the smoke room.

Martin opened the envelope and counted £45. The first thing he did was take his £10 out. He called Lisa and Kate over.

"Here are your tips Lisa, £10 for you and £10 for Kate. Sandra and

Nasser have also got a fiver each, but I don't think you should tell them you got anything," smiled Martin. Lisa nodded.

At about 10.55am, Sandra and Nasser emerged and Nasser seemed to be in a foul mood.

The waiters were just finishing laying the tables when Sandra came across with their money. They signed, got their money, said their farewells and left.

"Have you ripped me off?" snorted Nasser.

"I would not do that," said Sandra.

"You'd better not or you'll be out of a job. Don't open the next brown envelope you get until I get here, okay? Do you hear me? I'm telling you, it had better be the usual next Friday."

"Maybe Juan did not have any change, Nasser."

"Rubbish."

Lisa looked across at Kate, who was trying to keep a straight face, and smiled.

"Thanks guys," she murmured.

"Hi Mick, its Martin here. We pulled the switch with the courier's envelope. I think it is time to tell Georgio about the scam they are running."

"Okay Martin. I will call in the bar tonight and put Georgio in the picture, he will probably get rid of them. He would keep more staff if he does. That Sandra is a nasty piece of work."

"Mick, I think that job would be tailor made for our Nathan, full time breakfast manager. I know he's looking for a full time job and he does not enjoy working for cash in hand now that he's in a stable relationship with Jenny. Have a word with Georgio and I will speak to Nathan."

"That sounds good Martin. We put Nathan in and he books us for plenty of work, he would become our boss, so to speak, and the girls, Lisa and Kate, would like him."

"Ring us tomorrow and let us know how Georgio reacts."

"See you later Martin. Bye.

That night Mick and Chris called in to see Georgio in his usual place, the staff bar.

"Hi Mick, hi Chris, what are you having?" said Georgio as the two guys approached the bar.

"Just a couple of cokes Georgio, we're off to a little job in Harrogate. I just called in to give you a bit of information about your head waiter and restaurant supervisor. They are both in the Musicians Union."

"The Musicians Union? Mick, what do you mean?"

'They are both on the fiddle, that's what I mean."

"How, Mick?"

"You know the couriers always leave a brown envelope with a tip for the staff for looking after them during their two day stay?"

"I know that and it is shared out among the restaurant staff."

"No, Georgio. It is shared out between Nasser and Sandra and every couple of months they give the staff a fiver each. That is why you never have staff staying. They are being ripped off. We are talking about £75 every week during the summer months, three tours a week, £25 a tour."

"How did you rumble it, Mick?"

"Martin did yesterday, but I would rather not say how he did it but you can rest assured on Friday morning they will be at it again with the other courier when he departs at 10.00am. Sandra gets the brown envelope and gives it to Nasser when he comes in at 10.30am. They go upstairs for a coffee and smoke and share the money."

"I will catch them Friday morning and they will be down the road," said Georgio angrily.

"Must go Georgio. I'll leave it with you and don't worry about a new breakfast manager, we have got one ready for you."

"Thanks Mick, see you later.

Mick and Chris left and headed up the ring road to work.

On Friday morning Georgio was in reception to see Sandra collect the brown envelope from the other courier, Pedro, as he departed with his Spanish tourists. He waited until Nasser came in and followed them upstairs.

"Hi Kate, tell Lisa to keep an eye on the door to the staff room," laughed Dan who was busy clearing the tables after breakfast.

"Why Dan?" asked Lisa'

"You'll see," shouted Martin.

Next thing the door flew open and Sandra stormed through, quickly followed by Nasser.

"You stupid bitch, you let those waiters con you," snarled Nasser.

"You're not leaving us are you?" asked Dan, "was it something I said?" "Where will we send your leaving gift Sandra?" laughed Lisa. If looks could kill everyone would have died then.

"Bye Nasser, bye Sandra," shouted Kate laughing.

Just then Georgio came through.

"When can our new breakfast manager start, Martin?"

"I'll let you know tomorrow," smiled Martin.

"Hiya is Nathan there?" said Martin.

"I'll get him Martin, he's upstairs hoovering," said Jenny

"Nathan! Nathan!" shouted Jenny, "your dad is on the phone."

"Okay, I'll take it up here. Hi dad, what's going down? I haven't heard from you for a while, I hope it's about work."

"Why? Are you not happy in the little job you have got?" asked Martin.

"Not really, the job's alright but my boss is a chancer. You will have heard of him, Malcolm? He is older than you, been around a long time, he crawls up to the boss, he thinks the building would fall down if he took a day off," said Nathan.

"I know who you mean Nathan, Malcolm - he has about ten faces, not two faced, about 60 now, short white hair, quite tall, he never was one of us, a bit like Derek Crook, selfish, a glory seeker, definitely not to be trusted."

"That's him alright, the quicker I am out of here the better, but I don't fancy going on the circuit with you lot again, but I must admit, I miss the buzz. Anyway why the phone call?" "I have a job for you that will suit you down to the ground, no nights, finish every day at about three or four, you will be main man, Breakfast Manager at "The Hydro.""

"I know "The Hydro", I pass it every day on my way to work at "The Brunswick". But don't they have a Tunisian called Nasser there as main man?"

"Not anymore Nathan, we fixed it, we have been doing breakfasts there and found out he and his second in command, a girl called Sandra, were ripping the rest of the staff off."

"How dad?" asked Nathan

"The old brown envelope from the courier."

"You didn't pull the switch again did you?"

"Yes Dan and I did, Nasser blamed Sandra for ripping him off, we paid the girls then told Georgio and he paid them off. Ha ha!"

"I thought you were with Harry and Jacks dodgy agency?"

"It's not dodgy anymore. Jack has the licence so everything is above board, but anyway this is a full time job for you, nothing to do with any agencies. I have spoken to Georgio and everything is okay. You can start as soon as you can, of course you will need some casual staff."

"The casual staff will be from Jacks agency that means the team. Have I got that right dad, I will be your boss?"

"Got it in one Nathan," said Martin

"I must talk it out with the wife, okay? I will ring you tonight"

"What did your dad want Nathan?" shouted Jenny.

"He has offered me a breakfast manager's job at "The Hydro," said Nathan, as he came downstairs.

"But you have got a job Nathan. You know you must be careful about your decision," said Jenny, apprehensively.

"I will have to have a talk with Georgio the manager first, to see what will be expected of me and of course the money which I expect to be a lot more than I am getting at "The Brunswick.""

"If I was you I would check with Dan, why don't you ring him, his number is in the book."

Nathan rang Dan.

"Hi Joan, its Nathan, is Dan in?"

"Hello Nathan, it's good to hear from you. How's Jenny, tell her I hope she is well. I will go and get him, he is dozing as usual on the chair," said Joan

"Dan, Dan, wake up! Nathan is on the phone."

"Hiya Nathan I was just having a doze, what's happening?"

"My dad phoned me about a job at "The Hydro". What do you think, should I go for it? I think he might have his own interests at work and you know that Harry is lurking somewhere in the background,*' said Nathan sounding worried.

"Don't sound so worried Nathan. The job is tailor made for you, you will be the main man. Harry and Jack and the team will be no problem. There are two lovely girls there, Lisa and Kate, make them up to supervisors then build up your own team and blow Harry and Jack out. Where is the problem? Use us until you are settled in.

Georgio will go along with that. Tell him what you intend to do. He lost a lot of staff because of the other two, maybe now they may want to come back, especially when they hear they will get a fair crack of the whip concerning tips. I hope I have been of help. The advice I will give you is go for it." "Thanks a lot Dan. I think I will take your advice if only to see my dad's face when I tell him I don't need him anymore. Ha ha!"

"Just one thing Nathan, why don't you bring Mick along when you go to see Georgio, they go back a long time together, you can always get him at "Maggie's" at about 11.30 until 12.00, after breakfast."

"I think I will do that. I will ring him tomorrow. Thanks again Dan." Nathan put the phone down and turned to his wife," I must give "The Brunswick" a weeks' notice, I am going upmarket!"

"Is that "Maggie's"? Could I speak to Mick, tell him it's Nathan."

"Hold on, he has just walked in. Mick Phone call, its Nathan," said Paul.

"Hi Nathan, you just caught me. I've just walked in, I've just finished breakfast at "The Hydro" and I'm doing a lunch at "The Gate.""

"That's why I am phoning you. Is it possible you could come with me to "The Hydro" tomorrow to see Georgio about the breakfast manager's job?"

"No problem, I am there tomorrow morning anyway, they are short staffed, and we had to get rid of a couple, ha ha! Come at about 11.00am. I will introduce you to the man, but I will have to rush off at about 11.30 as I am taking my two boys up to the park for a game of footie," said Mick.

'Thanks Mick, what ages are they now anyway?"

"One is ten and the other is eleven."

'Time flies, they were about five and six when I saw them last that was when their mother marched them into "The Gate" and left them in the reception and stormed off to Nottingham. Crazy woman that one."

"We are not together now but I see the boys as often as I can as long as she gets cash for bingo and nights out. See you tomorrow, bye."

When Nathan arrived at "The Hydro" Mick had just finished breakfast and was waiting by reception.

"Good morning Nathan, nice to see you, let's go and meet Georgio."

"What do I call him Mick?"

"His name is Mr Bianco but he prefers to be called Georgio," said Mick

"Come in, you must be Nathan. Mick has told me you could be the man to sort out my restaurant," said Georgio, sitting back with his hands behind his head.

"I do hope so, Mr Bianco"

"Just call me Georgio, everybody does. As you can see here, we have a very busy hotel, mostly tours but we have quite a few celebrities and T V people who stay. We also do a lot of weddings in the summer and small conferences in the winter. I have known Mick a long time and he reckons you will be able to run my restaurant in the mornings. I do have a restaurant manager who comes on at lunchtime. He is Italian and has been a friend of mine for many years. You will like him, he is called Giovanni."

"I will have to give a week's notice at my present job so I would be able to start Thursday week," said Nathan.

"That is okay with me, see you then," said Georgio as they walked to the door.

'Thanks Mick. He seems a nice guy," said Nathan.

"Do you want a lift Nathan? I am going your way to pick the kids up."

"No Mick, I'm going into town to meet the wife, see you later."

With that they headed off in different directions. Nathan was highly delighted after all these years. The prospect of being his dad's boss was like a dream to him.

Next morning Martin and Dan arrived at the Hydro a bit late and there was no sign of Mick or Chris.

"Where is Mick and Chris, Lisa?" asked Dan "Don't know," answered Lisa. "Thank god it's not busy today or we would have been right in the shit," said Martin, "They have probably been out on the piss."

"But that's not like Mick. He never knocks, hangover or not," said Dan

"Give Chris a ring, Dan"

"Okay, I'll give them another 15 minutes."

At 7.30am Dan phoned Chris.

"What's happening Chris," said Dan

"I don't know where Mick is. His car is not outside his flat and if he doesn't come soon I won't be in. I'm at "The Gate" for lunch at 12.00 so I may have to make my own way there."

"Okay Chris, Martin and I are there today, give Joan a ring, she'll give you a lift, I will be going from here with Martin. See you in "Maggie's", bye."

"Martin, Chris won't be in, no sign of Mick, maybe that rubbish car has broken down but it is strange he did not ring."

"Anyway, let's get the job done and get our money and get off to "The Gate" for the lunch."

They got to "Maggie's" at about 11.45am. Chris and Joan were already there.

"Hi, any phone calls from Mick this morning."

"Just Harry, he said he was coming here this morning, he seemed upset"

"He probably had to pay out money," laughed Joan.

About 10 minutes later the door opened and in walked Harry with Jack behind him.

"A large whiskey," said Harry

"Are you sure Harry," asked Paul, surprised

"Yes."

Joan looked around the team in the corner, the look of shock to see Harry order a large whiskey, something was wrong. Jack had his arm around Harry. Harry looked like he was crying.

"Something's happened,'" said Dan to Chris.

Harry and Jack walked over to the corner where the team were sitting.

"I have some bad news for you all. Mick has had an accident, I have been at the hospital all night," he slumped down on his seat and drank back his whiskey.

"What happened Harry? How is he?" asked Dan

"It seems yesterday afternoon he picked his kids up and went to the park to play football, of course he called at the off licence for a four pack of special brew. He played for a while then sat down to enjoy his lager. One of the kids hit the ball up a tree. Mick climbed up to get it and fell off. The eldest boy phoned an ambulance.

Mick could not move his legs. I got a call last night from Pinderfields Hospital. They found my number in his clothes."

"Is he going to be alright?" asked Joan.

'The doctors can't be sure but he may not be able to walk again," said Harry.

Chris had tears in his eyes, Mick and Chris had been very close for years. Everyone was devastated. The word went around "Maggie's". Waiters and waitresses from other hotels who used the bar were shocked. Mick was highly thought of by everyone.

Darren at "The River Gate" was deeply shocked, and the lunch that the team were working on for him was a very sombre lunch. Everyone's thoughts were of Mick, his kids and whether he could ever walk again. When the lunch finished, everyone went across to "Maggie's".

Darren said he would phone Pinderfields Hospital and come across and let people know the news.

Everyone seemed to be there, even some of the full time staff from other departments had gathered, all concerned about their friend. About half an hour later Darren came in and you could have heard a pin drop.

"I have just been in contact with Pinderfields Hospital and have been informed that Mick is in Ward 6 and has regained consciousness, preliminary tests have shown he has broken his back. His chances of ever walking again are very slim and if so only with the aid of sticks. They have asked if he could be left to rest for a few days before people visit him. His sons and his girlfriend are with him at the moment you all know how I feel, thanks for your time, I'm too upset to say anything else."

With that he turned to Chris, gave him a hug, turned and went back to "The River Gate".

Nobody spoke. Everyone either went back to work or made their way home except Martin, Chris, Dan and Joan. Harry and Jack stood at the bar. Chris was the first to speak.

"You all know how close Chris and I were. He taught me all I know. In fact he carried me in many jobs. On hearing this news today, I feel I have lost my right arm."

With that he stood up, took his dickie bow off, put it on the table, turned around and with tears in his eyes announced, "I have just done my last job as a waiter. Harry, any money owed to me put it towards a collection for Mick. Goodbye my friends, thanks for the many great memories."

With tears running down his face he walked out the door without looking back.

On the way home Dan and Joan were both thinking about Mick and all the times he came out of his way to pick them up in his clapped out cars. They both felt sad about how he had deteriorated over the last couple of years with booze and how he had to work twice as hard to keep up.

"We must go over and see him Dan," said Joan

"I agree, let's go tonight, your mam can look after James," agreed Dan.

When they arrived at the hospital Dan asked the receptionist for directions to Ward 6. "Along the corridor to the end and turn left," said the receptionist.

"Remember Mick won't know how badly hurt he is, so don't say anything Dan."

"I am not that stupid," said Dan

"There he is, in the comer, that's his girlfriend and her sister with him. Be prepared for a few dramatics," said Joan

"How are you feeling Mick? I have seen you looking better," said Dan trying to cheer him up.

"I have to lay flat for about six weeks and try not to move. It seems I have damaged my spine when I fell," said Mick. "I still cannot feel my legs, the doctor says the feeling might come back in time."

"Let's hope so Mick, let's hope so," said Dan glancing across at Joan who had tears in her eyes.

"We'd better get off Mick. I have to collect the boys, see you tomorrow, I will bring clean pyjamas and some fruit, nice to see you again Joan, bye."

"I'm glad she has gone," said Mick, "all I got out of her was 'what am I going to do for money'" Here I am lying here on my back hoping for some sort of miracle and she walks in." Just then the nurse arrived and asked them to leave as she wanted Mick to get some rest.

'Tell Harry and Jack not to put me on breakfast for a few days," laughed Mick.

"Anything you need, get the nurse to give us a ring Mick. We will come again next week," said Joan.

When they got home the answer phone was full of enquiries about Mick. Joan made some coffee and Dan began returning the calls.

"Do you get the feeling things will not be the same again?" asked Joan

"It's strange you said that Joan, I have been thinking that all day," sighed Dan.

After a couple of months in hospital Mick got a flat on his own and his drinking accelerated. He kept falling out of his wheelchair. It became too painful to visit him.

Dan tried to get him to go to AA with him but he said he enjoyed his special brews and made it clear people in the team who came to visit him were not welcome.

"If he wants us to visit him let him ring us," Dan announced one morning in "Maggie's". He clearly does not want us to call. I think it tears him apart to see us leaving to go to work. The last time I visited him he was down and when I left he called after me with tears in his eyes, 'I still have my memories Dan, we were the best, thanks."

"I have been in touch with his brothers in Glasgow and they are coming down to bring him home," said Harry. "His girlfriend has taken his sons with her to Nottingham where she comes from."

A couple of weeks later, Joan mentioned to Dan," I passed Mick's flat this morning and it was boarded up, Dan, looks like he has gone home to Glasgow."

"Let's hope he goes to AA in Glasgow," said Dan hopefully.

"Good morning everyone, this is Nathan, your new Breakfast Manager," announced Giovanni. As you know I do not work until 11.30am so Nathan will be my eyes and ears, he comes highly recommended so I hope you give him your full co-operation."

"Hello, I'm Nathan. Thank you Giovanni, I see we are well staffed. I know Dan over there and Billy and Jean. You must be Lisa and Kate."

"I'm Lisa and that's Kate," said Lisa, pointing across to Kate. "Mick told us you would be starting, we heard from Dan about the accident, we sent some flowers to the hospital, hope he recovers."

"Hi Dan, I won't be doing any work today, just sorting rotas and getting to know people," said Nathan.

"I bet you are looking forward to being your dad's boss, Nathan," laughed Dan, "he is at "The Gate" today but he will be here tomorrow morning."

"Do you know, Dan, I have waited years to tell him what to do in a restaurant. When I think of all those years of 'Nathan, not that way', 'Are you stupid, how many times have I told you...' Now I have finally got my chance tell him" smiled Nathan.

"I know he was a hard task master Nathan, but he in my mind is the best, a professional, not many about in this business now, mostly cowboys. You would not be breakfast manager here, and this is a four star, at your age 24, had it not been for him."

"I learnt more from you and Mick, but to be honest he did teach me a lot. It won't stop me getting him to polish those windows and clean that carvery tomorrow," laughed Nathan.

The next morning Billy, Jean and Dan arrived at 6.45am. Lisa and Kate were busy putting the butters and milks on the tables. Nathan was talking to the breakfast chef. Dan headed as usual to the coffee machine. Billy and Jean began turning the cups up on the tables.

"Where's Martin?" Nathan asked Dan.

"I don't know, I thought he would be here by now. Perhaps he has changed his mind thinking you would give him a hard time," laughed Dan.

"Rubbish I saw him in "Maggie's" last night and he was looking forward to working under you Nathan," said Billy. "Whatever it is, it must be important, he will be here soon."

At about 8.00am, the phone rang and Kate answered it.

"Nathan! Phone. I think it is Martin"

"Where are you dad? What do you mean you won't be in? Speak up! I can't hear you, say that again."

"I have just won a fifth share in last night's lottery, about £400,000 pounds"

ABOUT THE AUTHOR

Donal worked in the catering business for 40 years, during that time he came across various characters and recently decided to put pen to paper. He lives in Leeds, with his son. He is a Reiki Master/Teacher. Reiki principles have been his passion for the last 15 years.

ISBN: 1500979708
ISBN-13: 9781500979706